Praise for Natural Remote

*This highly informative and easy t
a perfect first step for anyone who is interested in
learning the art of remote viewing but doesn't know
where to begin. I assign this as mandatory reading for
my own classes.*

Debra Lynne Katz
Director of **The International School of Clairvoyance**, and author
**You Are Psychic: The Art of Clairvoyant Reading & Healing
Extraordinary Psychic: Proven Techniques to Master Your Natural Abilities
Freeing the Genie Within**

*With this remarkable little book, Jon gives anyone with
the desire to try remote viewing the foundation and the
tools needed to begin their own exploration of the
wonders of the human mind. As the wise have always
said....Know thyself.*

Mary Crosby, RVPGNYC member

*Terrific, short intro to RV, the au natural way....I think
using this guide virtually anyone can learn how to
transcend space and time and view the unimaginable.*

Berl Kaufman, RVPGNYC member, Amazon review

*If someone asked me how to get started in RV, I would
recommend this book to them.*

Brandon Jepson, Amazon review

*...a fantastic introduction book for the newbie/student
of remote viewing. Packed with tips and great advice
for the novice giving them much needed advice to try
this mental martial art for themselves.*

Darryl Smith, Amazon review

Natural Remote Viewing

A practical guide to the mental martial
art of self-discovery

2nd Edition
Revised and Expanded

Jon Noble

Foreword by Pam Coronado

INTENTI NAL
PRESS

Intentional Press
Box 2636, Cedar City, Utah 84720
editor@intentionalpress.com
intentionalpress.com
(866) 229-7847

ISBN 978-1-938815-03-4

Second edition

Contents

Foreword

I can't actually recall when I first met Jon Noble because we've both been traveling the same remote viewing circle for years. When I became President of the International Remote Viewing Association in 2013, Jon was, and still is, running IRVA's free target practice forum, Focal Point. I bring this up, first to acknowledge his dedication and hard work and second, to remind readers that he is an experienced teacher. During a conference a few years ago, we held a raffle in which many speakers and authors graciously donated their books. This is when I first learned of Jon's book "Natural Remote Viewing: A Practical Guide to the Mental Martial Art of Self-Discovery." I was thrilled to see this handy, practical guide because it filled a significant gap. Now here I am writing the foreword for his second edition.

During my term at IRVA, I became keenly aware of the need for more accessible and affordable "how to" guides for remote viewing. While there is an abundance of information out there about remote viewing and the fascinating history, there is little written about the actual process, especially the less formal, natural form of RV. I was a natural intuitive long before I became trained in the more structured CRV method which is why I appreciate Jon's approach and easy to navigate guide. For those who want to learn at home, this book is the perfect solution.

Pam Coronado

Preface to the Second Edition

As a self-professed non-psychic, with nothing to relate in terms of personal psi experiences, the remote viewing training I took in 2010 with Russell Targ and Stephan Schwartz had a profound effect on me. Here was something that was not really spoken about, suddenly being presented as if it were a normal, everyday affair; their message was matter of fact and simple: remote viewing is possible - we used it to find things - here is a simple procedure - now go and practise.

What I experienced that week convinced me that I did indeed have some small psychic ability, and that the remote viewing approach held an opportunity for fellow psychically challenged individuals to gain some direct experience, as I had, of the phenomena of psi.

Why doesn't everyone know about this? I started a practice group to spread the word and, over the years of running it, I found myself repeating remote viewing's fundamentals - its definition, protocols, and methods - to new members. *Why don't I write this down?*, I wondered. By doing so, I could *literally* spread the word.

These were the seeds of the first edition of this book. I wanted to produce a concise and straightforward introduction, which could be understood by those unfamiliar with what remote viewing was or how to perform it; something easily digestible, which would spur them on to try it for themselves and, hopefully, gain first-hand experience of *being psychic*.

Although I felt this goal was generally met, in review, there was more to say: some concepts could have been better explained and developed. And things do not stay the same. I've read more books, attended more meetings, completed more courses and hopefully learnt from my own remote viewing successes and failures.

We each experience reality in our own way; we each have our own filters and experiences that we use to measure and relate new information against. This makes the explanation of anything to those who have not experienced it for themselves difficult at the best of times, and especially true for something as ineffable as distinguishing psychic information from mind chatter, imagination, memory and conjecture: the artefacts of our keen analytical, albeit often random, thought processes.

So, here is a second edition with more emphasis on the importance of intention in the remote viewing process, and the feeling/knowing experience of the remote viewer.

Much of the book has been revised; new information and new tools are provided, including a method to describe the surrounding locale of the remote viewing target based on a process outlined by Pam Coronado, a vocabulary of adjectives, a simplified model of consciousness to help explain the concepts on which the remote viewing method is based, and an expanded history of remote viewing in the United States. All of this has passed through my own filters and should be viewed as one set of thoughts on a human ability that is far from being understood.

One topic has been removed: local sidereal time. At the time of the first edition's publication, the viewer's local sidereal time was thought to be a factor in the accuracy of remote viewing; I added it as a point of interest, but stated that it should not impede the viewer's practice. Subsequent analysis, based on a much larger data set, by the author of the original paper, has now dispelled its impact on remote viewing. As such, the viewer does not need to concern him/herself with it.

Introduction

Institutional science has no explanation for what is referred to as psi phenomena[1] and so, against its own principle of investigation to acquire knowledge, takes the position that such phenomena are not worthy of study. As such phenomena don't fit our current models of physics they cannot exist, therefore they don't exist.

Experimenters that state they do are branded as practising pseudo-science; they are deluding themselves, seeing effects from mere coincidence. Another approach to make the problem go away is to state experiments that show an effect are flawed, and where no flaws can be found even going to the extent of stating that not enough time has passed to be able to uncover them, as in the case of the *Evaluation of Remote Viewing AIR* report.[2]

These responses have been the standard reply to decades of replicated studies of remote viewing and the similar 'ganzfeld' experiment.

Unfortunately, this tactic extends to anything that questions the existing paradigm. Claims of psychic abilities are proclaimed as irrational, ungrounded in fact and reality and, for some stuck in their dogma from the Dark Ages, even demonic. The message here is that the topic of psychic abilities and those who profess them should be shunned and ridiculed; *there's nothing to see here*.

As well as a missed opportunity for science, this stance is impeding the growth of society in general by impeding the growth of the individual.

Denying over a 100 years of compelling psi anecdotes and replicated scientific studies limits and blinds us to our true potential. The reality of statistically significant results from the meta-analysis of multiple remote viewing[3,4], ganzfeld studies, and other free-response psi experiments[5] that span decades, show that the materialistic/physicalistic views of the world are incomplete (surely an area of investigation for the true scientist). We are truly more than our physical bodies and have access to information beyond that available to our physical senses.

For those who believe themselves not to be psychic, with little tangible experience of this other world, this reality is not readily apparent. Thus, accepting the cynics' 'nothing to see here' view is an understandable and easy solution, allowing the paranormal to be put aside allowing the world of the physical senses to continue uninterrupted. But the paranormal pervades our stories and myths; commonplace material for novels and TV programmes. Stories from family, friends and acquaintances tell of futures foretold, strangers met, knowledge of distressed loved ones from across vast distances,[6] accounts of missed journeys due to 'having a bad feeling' resulting in miraculous escapes from danger,[7] and even studies showing a correlation between precognition abilities of executives and their company's performance.[8]

Are all these coincidences? Or do some offer a glimpse into a larger reality that is not bound by physical constraints?

A straightforward and accessible way for the individual to experience this other world and this greater potential for themselves is offered by the remote viewing protocols and procedures.

Much of what we currently call 'remote viewing' is available to us today in large part due to the United States Government, and the work carried out under its auspices from 1972 until 1995, the latter part of the Cold War period. Concerned with a possible 'psi gap' with the Russians (equivalent to the 'missile gap', the perceived disparity in firepower between the superpowers), the CIA initiated a programme to investigate the outlandish reports coming from behind the Iron Curtain. Could the enemy read their minds and control their equipment? *Surely there was nothing to it? But if there was, how could we use it?*

California's Stanford Research Institute (SRI) was the ideal place to secretly study the phenomena or rather, as expected, prove that the soviets were just wasting their money; the organization had established ties with the CIA and, in Hal Puthoff, a scientist receptive to investigating psychic phenomena. Laser physicist Russell Targ joined shortly afterwards, and work began on exploring the limits of remote viewing and identifying the characteristics of individuals with a talent for it.

In 1977, the United States Army saw remote viewing as a potential threat to military installations and recruited psychics from within its ranks to test it for themselves. Later, this effort turned towards using remote viewing as an intelligence gathering tool.

Between the two programmes here was a resolute attempt, running for more than 20 years, to scientifically measure and quantify psychic functioning, as well as use it as an intelligence gathering tool. These endeavours, which have since become known as Project Star Gate (although this was the last name, of a list of many, for the operational arm in the military), established the remote viewing protocols and procedures that make up the core of what is practised today.

Even with its top-secret status, the programme published several scientific papers, enabling others to use their practices and attempt to replicate their results.

Outside of the government programme, major participants in this new era of research and use of psychic abilities included the Princeton Engineering Anomalies Research (PEAR) lab, which used the SRI model as a basis for further research, and Stephan Schwartz' Mobius Society, which focused on the application of psychic abilities in a variety of areas, including archaeology, picking stocks and in the search for missing people. (The history section at the back of the book aims to provide a high-level overview of the period.)

A hypothesis of the researchers at SRI was that psychic abilities are distributed throughout the population, in the same way as many other human talents, in a bell curve; a few are gifted, and some have very little aptitude, while most of us are somewhere in the middle. Targ and Puthoff were sufficiently confident of this, that when asked to demonstrate what progress the programme was making, they would cast those making the request in the role of the psychic. Here, visitors, there to ensure that funds were not being fraudulently wasted, found themselves in the role of the remote viewer, and more surprisingly (and difficult to explain to their colleagues back at the office) producing evidence of their own psychic abilities.

What better way to prove something than by direct experience?

The remote viewing methodologies used and refined at SRI, and by others during this period, provide the tools and a structure with which to have access to direct experiences of psychic functioning. This guide attempts to capture the essence of these, such that, given time, a little effort and focused intention, you can too.

Remote Viewing Basics

What Is Remote Viewing?

Remote viewing is a form of extrasensory perception (ESP), it has, however, some distinguishing features that differentiate it from other forms of psychic functioning such as spontaneous psychic impressions, out-of-body experiences and mediumship.

Remote viewing is a *structured* use of the natural psychic abilities latent in all of us. 'Structured use' implies employing these innate abilities through the use of particular *methods*, for predefined and specific *purposes*, within specific *protocols*.

A definition of remote viewing needs to address each of these elements: *purpose*, *protocol* and *method* to fully define what remote viewing is. The trainee practitioner needs to acquire knowledge and experience of these fundamentals through training and practice to call themselves a remote viewer.

Purpose

The definition of remote viewing from the Defense Intelligence Agency's *Coordinate Remote Viewing Training Manual* reads:

> *...the acquisition and description, by mental means, of information blocked from ordinary perception by distance, shielding, or time.*[9]

This is performed by making contact, psychically, with the area of interest and probing it for information, whilst capturing the experience in words and sketches. The result and purpose of remote viewing is the recorded descriptive information. This ability to describe can be applied to people, places, things and events, and can be used in finding lost items, and as distance and time seem to have little bearing on its effectiveness, foretelling future events or investigating the past. In other words, describing anything, at any time.

Remote viewing speaks less in symbols and metaphor, as sometimes used in mediumship, or tarot card reading, but in tangible description. It aims for the accuracy of detailed and specific information.

Remote viewing can be applied in a number of areas: Initially, the remote viewer will work through training targets as part of learning the skill; and, once familiar with the process and producing good information, they may progress to actually using remote viewing as a tool. Historically the uses of remote viewing have been classified as either being *operational* or *research*.

- ⊙ Remote viewing for the purposes of gathering useful information is known as *'operational'*. Examples of such projects could include finding a lost item, researching a historical event, describing a new technology, or predicting the outcome of a future event.

- ⊙ *Research* projects investigate and test the limits of remote viewing itself under controlled conditions. For example, much of the work carried out at the PEAR, SRI, and Science Applications International Corporation (SAIC) labs was focused on producing statistics to show an effect, and testing how different factors affected the quality of remote viewing.

Even the best and most experienced remote viewers maintain a consistent level of practice.

Protocol

The term 'remote viewing' implies the use of our natural psychic ability within a prescribed methodology, whilst conforming to protocols established at SRI during the United States Government-funded investigation and the operational use of psychic abilities. This study sought to place scientific controls around the psychic process in an effort to measure and understand it, with the goal of improving its effectiveness.

The following protocols are required for the practice to be called remote viewing:

- ⊙ Tasks are planned
- ⊙ The remote viewer is 'blind' to the target
- ⊙ Sessions are recorded
- ⊙ Feedback is available for training purposes

Tasks Are Planned

Remote viewing is performed with the intent of gaining information related to a predefined query. Prior to the remote itself, a remote viewing task is formulated that defines this request for information about a 'target'. A remote viewing target could be a location, an object, an event or a person - in fact, anything *blocked from ordinary perception*, as far as the remote viewer is concerned, *by distance, shielding or time.*

The process starts with the tasker, the person setting the task, defining the information they require and documenting this request in a clearly worded manner, unambiguous in its intent and meaning. This documented request states the tasker's intent for information. The tasker then assigns what is known as a target reference number (TRN) - a short series of random numbers and letters - to the task (more on this later). This allows the task to be assigned to the viewer, without informing them what the task is, this meets the requirement that the viewer is 'blind' to the target. The viewer's intent is to satisfy the tasker's request by following a remote viewing procedure to access and record the required information.

The Remote Viewer Is 'Blind' to the Target

An important remote viewing protocol is that the viewer is 'blind' to the target, meaning the viewer should not be told anything about it, in terms of what the task is or even the topic of the enquiry.

Although this may sound like a hindrance, blindness to the target inhibits interference from the viewer's analytical mind, such as analysis and guessing. It is difficult to discern between the processes of analysis and classification that we use to navigate through our physical world, the random noise of our thoughts and true psychic information, but doing so is the key to remote viewing.

If you were asked to make a prediction on whether the stock market was to go up or down, you would find this difficult to accomplish without your thoughts on the state of the economy coming to mind. The thinking, reasoning part of your mind naturally wants to step in and help answer the question. Even if you consciously tried not to, some part of you would weigh things up and take a view. This is how we navigate the world; we answer everyday questions or issues by working through them analytically, based on the information available to us at the time.

The remote viewing protocol of viewer blindness to the target attempts to minimize this analytical interference by not giving you any clues as to the subject of the enquiry; you only have your psychic abilities to rely on for information.

In research and some operational projects, blindness is taken a step further to include everyone involved with the viewer - anyone in the same room as the viewer is also 'blind' to the target. This is known as a 'double-blind'.

Front-loading

If the viewer does know something about the target beforehand, this is known as the viewer being 'front-loaded'. This is generally not optimal for the reasons described above, but there are exceptions. Sometimes it is unavoidable, and experienced and talented viewers can still perform well. Also, in some situations, such as in learning how to remote view and practice exercises, an indication as to the type of target may help the viewer focus on the sort of information required. An example of acceptable front-loading would be to specify the type of target, such as 'the target is a person'. Being front-loaded with anything more specific than this will give the analytical thought processes too much information to work with, allowing conjecture to build and compete with psychic information.

The paper, *Remote Viewing the Outcome of the 2012 Presidential Election* (Katz & Bulgatz, 2013), contains a discussion on the meaning of 'blindness' in research projects generally, and the need to use front-loading in this particular project.

Sessions Are Recorded

If it's not written down, it doesn't count! The remote viewer is required to write their impressions of the target as they are perceived.

The viewer's name and location, as well as the date and the time should also be documented.

Most remote viewing sessions are recorded by being written down by the viewer at the time, but audio and video recording can also be used (many recorded video sessions can now be found online).

Feedback Is Available for Remote Viewing Training

Feedback is usually in the form of photographs, with some description of the target; but it could also include audio or video content, physical objects, or a combination of these. It should be provided to the viewer only after they have completed their session.

Feedback provides evidence that there was psychic functioning, without which it would be difficult, if not impossible, to claim that any remote viewing actually took place. Remote viewing the dark side of the moon may make for an interesting target (and it does; see Ingo Swann's book *Penetration*); but, without a reliable source of information to measure against, it is impossible to gauge at what level the remote viewer's session is correct and how much imagination played a part in the process. Therefore, it is essential for training purposes that verifiable targets, with good feedback materials, are selected.

It is the tasker's responsibility to provide the target feedback, although, once the target is known, the viewer can research it for themselves. Often, there are details that the viewer recorded on their session transcript, which are not shown on the tasker-supplied feedback. It is good practice for the viewer to investigate and confirm their own perceptions of the target.

Successful remote viewing is not dependent on feedback being available. There are examples of accurate sessions where feedback was not seen by the viewer. However, new and practising viewers should always review the feedback against their session transcript, as it is an important part of the process of learning remote viewing. As such, good feedback should always be available for training and practice targets.

Methods of Remote Viewing

Many cultures and spiritual traditions have psychic practices. Listed here, however, are the methods used and refined in the United States since the 1970s.

There are several methods of remote viewing available. Some are more structured and require a greater investment of time to learn, while others, such as the one outlined in this book, are less formal. Each contains tools designed to help the process of remote viewing. Each produces results. The individual needs to determine what seems most suitable for their purposes.

'Targ/Schwartz' / Natural Remote Viewing

Known by several names, including simply 'remote viewing', this is a less formal approach which involves the viewer 'quietening' their mind (an invitation to the viewer, as described by Russell Targ to 'sit down and shut up'), mentally accessing the target by bringing their awareness to it, and recording their perceptions.

Although the viewer is free to use their own methods the following should be incorporated: open questioning that allows for free-response answers, sketching, all senses are queried, and importantly, a focus on target description and not identification, with a visual separation between responses believed to be psychic perceptions from those believed to be analysis and conjecture.

The viewer is free to use their own format of recording the session.

Such personal approaches can be referred to as remote viewing as long as the remote viewing protocols are met. This guide provides a procedure for this type of remote viewing, although I have also provided a prescribed method and a suggested format for recording the session.

Such methods were used exclusively in the early days at SRI, and throughout the government-funded programme, as well as operationally in the United States military. Joe McMoneagle, Russell Targ and Stephan Schwartz describe this style of remote viewing and the projects it was used in within their books. Schwartz and McMoneagle continue to teach it today.

Controlled Remote Viewing

Controlled remote viewing (CRV) is a formal and structured procedure with several distinct stages that build upon each other. Developed at SRI by Ingo Swann, a gifted natural psychic, and Hal Puthoff in the early 1980s, it was an attempt at defining a teachable remote viewing procedure modelled on Swann's own process. Incorporating learning theory and other psychological thinking of the time, including elements of Neuro-linguistic programming (NLP), CRV uses a set of its own terminology, conceptual models and theory to explain the process.

Swann trained the United States military in the new method, which produced the *Coordinate Remote Viewing Training Manual* quoted earlier (Coordinate being the initial 'C' in CRV, later changed to Controlled). This document is now available online (see the 'Websites' section), although it was never intended to be a standalone instruction manual.

Several variants of CRV have been produced following Swann's original, with different instructors providing their own interpretation and additions.[10] Various training options are available, including self-study books, video, online courses and classroom training. The recommended approach would be to receive classroom training with an established organization or experienced individual. Several of the original military remote viewers provide such training opportunities.

There is some debate over the effectiveness of CRV as compared to non-CRV approaches. There has been little in the way of a head-to-head comparison except that performed at SRI itself, which showed an improvement in a remote viewer's data accuracy from 22% before to 66% after CRV training.[11] Issue 13 of the *eight martinis* magazine contains an article by Daz Smith on this topic that includes an interview with Hal Puthoff.

For some, CRV is thought of as the only remote viewing method, to the exclusion of others; it should be noted, however, that the SRI programme had been running for several years prior to the development of CRV and that some of remote viewing's outstanding successes, that kept the programme funded during this period, came from using non-CRV methods. Similarly, Schwartz' archaeological and other Mobius projects, PEAR Lab's research, and Ed May's work at the Science Applications International Corporation (SAIC) did not use CRV.

Hawaii Remote Viewers' Guild

Hawaii Remote Viewers' Guild (HRVG) is a formal, structured procedure with several steps. It was developed in the early 1980s by United States Army Special Forces working with noted psychic Dr. Richard Ireland. Like CRV it also incorporated some of the concepts of NLP. The method has produced excellent results. For more information, visit the HRVG online (see the 'Websites' section).

Extended Remote Viewing

Extended remote viewing (ERV) requires the viewer to get into a hypnagogic state, most readily achieved by the viewer being very relaxed, lying down in comfortable, quiet surroundings. Once the required state has been reached, the viewer is verbally prompted by someone else, known as a 'monitor', for information, to which the viewer verbally responds. As the viewer is not in a position to write during the session as in the other methods, sound recordings and the monitor's notes become the record. These can be supplemented with notes and sketches made by the viewer after the session.

This method was used in the military, particularly in its early involvement with remote viewing. It also has some similarities to the process used by Edgar Cayce, known as 'The Sleeping Prophet', the 20th century's most well-documented psychic.

Dream Remote Viewing

Reports of precognitive information, ideas and creative inspiration coming from dreams are common. The dream state and the threshold states between being asleep and awake are natural times where the analytical processes are suppressed, providing a more receptive environment for creative and precognitive impressions to flourish.

Paul McCartney woke one morning with the tune *Yesterday* in his head. Author Richard Bach claims that the ending of his book *Jonathan Livingston Seagull* came to him in a dream after an eight-year hiatus. Larry Page dreamt about the concepts behind the

Google search engine. Elias Howe, inventor of the sewing machine, was shown the configuration needed for the needles in a dream. Friedrich Kekule stated the structure of the benzene molecule came to him in a dream.

As well as reports from individuals receiving information in dreams, various studies have shown the ability of dreamers to describe a predefined target. The most well-known studies were carried out at the Dream Laboratory at the Maimonides Medical Center in New York. Montague Ullman established the centre in 1962 'to explore the problem of telepathy and dreams by means of the newly discovered rapid eye movement (REM) monitoring technique.'[12] Experiments tasked sleepers to dream about an image being 'sent' by another person. A meta-analysis of the 1,270 Maimonides Dream Laboratory and related trials found the overall hit rate to be 59.1%,[13] whereas 50% would be expected by chance. According to Dean Radin in *Entangled Minds*, his comprehensive overview of psi research; 'This 9.1% increase over chance may not sound like much, but it's associated with odds against chance of 22 billion to 1. This rules out coincidence as a variable explanation.'[14]

Building on a previous informal experiment concerning his own ability to dream about a future news story photograph,[15] which showed an effect, Dale Graff has recently worked with remote viewer Patricia Cyrus on an experiment to describe a future photograph-of-the-day from his local newspaper's 'Around the World' section. The project used remote viewing in both the conscious and dream states (Dale refers to these as 'Conscious State Psi' and 'Dream State Psi', respectively). At the time the remote viewing was performed, the incident or event that was photographed *had not yet happened*. The photographs were not published in Dale's newspaper until three days after the sessions. There is a clear correspondence between the remote viewing sketches and the targets shown in the published write-up of the experiments. In blind judging, the descriptions of the day's photograph were detailed and accurate enough to be called a 'hit' for 64% of the 33 sessions performed (with a 'p' value of 0.04).[16]

Inspired by Graff and Cyrus' success and the work of the Maimonides Dream Laboratory, Nancy Smith, Debra Katz and Michelle Bulgatz designed a dream-based associative remote viewing (ARV) experiment.[17] As ARV can be used to predict the outcome of events, it provides a clear measure of accuracy, in terms of how many predications are correct.

The 'Sweet Dreams' project measured the accuracy of predictions of the outcome of future sports events derived from the ability of dreamers to describe an image associated with the winning team. In 50 trials, the winning team was predicted 33 times.

The Sweet Dreams team was made up of an experienced group of remote viewers who had been working together on a regular basis for five years. They felt that dream state psi was much richer, more colourful, more story-driven and more detailed than their experience of conscious state psi. The project also saw viewers receiving information about each other. On more than one occasion specific information, not related to the target, but to the viewers themselves, showed up on several transcripts.[18]

To dream about a target, you will need to establish your intention by writing the target number (or however the target has been specified, for example, 'main photograph on tomorrow's front page') down and saying it to yourself several times during the day. This will inform your consciousness that you are serious about dreaming about it. Then focus on the target as you fall asleep.

Dream impressions, images and sensations need to be recorded directly as you awaken. Moving around to any extent when you wake up will dislodge the memories of your dream, so ensure that you have the necessary materials to record your dreams by your bedside, ready, close at hand. The habit of recording your dreams, as you awake, will help with remembering them.

The proliferation of smartphones and dream journaling software is making the recording and data mining of these dreams more practical.

'What is Remote Viewing?' Section Summary

Remote viewing is the structured use of the natural psychic ability, latent in all of us, to retrieve information *blocked from ordinary perception by distance, shielding or time*. 'Structured use' refers to the fact the practice has a predefined *purpose*, *method*, and, most importantly, adheres to established remote viewing *protocols*:

- ✓ Tasks are planned
- ✓ Sessions are recorded
- ✓ The viewer is blind to the target
- ✓ Feedback is available for training purposes

⊙ Following remote viewing training, viewers could offer their skills for operational and research projects. A level of ongoing practice should be maintained.

⊙ Remote viewing is an intent-driven practice that starts with the tasker's intent to know some information. The remote viewer's intention is to satisfy the tasker's request by following a remote viewing procedure to retrieve the requested information.

⊙ Several methods of remote viewing are available – including variants of controlled remote viewing and other structured methods, to the more free-form non-CRV methods.

⊙ The **tasker** is the person requesting information. The tasker creates the task, generates the target reference number, sources the feedback and assigns the task to the viewer.

⊙ The **task** is the tasker's documented request for information. Tasks must be clearly and unambiguously defined.

⊙ The **target reference number** (TRN), also known as the 'target coordinate', is a short series of random numbers and letters assigned to the task by the tasker. By hiding the actual description of the task, the TRN enables the task to be assigned to the viewer whilst retaining viewer blindness.

- The **target** is the object of the task, as defined by the tasker.

- **'Blind'** refers to the remote viewing protocol that the viewer should not know what the task or target is. Even the topic, or area of query, should not be known. 'Double-blind', used in research projects, calls for all involved with the viewer, including those assigning the target to the viewer, to be blind as well.

- **'Front-loading'** is where the viewer is informed of some aspect of the target prior to performing their session. Too much front-loaded information is likely to cause the viewer to be presented with artefacts from their own memory and imagination. Limited front-loading, such as specifying the type of target (e.g., 'the target is a location'), can be useful under certain circumstances, including training.

- A **remote viewing session** is the period of time and the resulting output of the time that the viewer spends remote viewing the target.

- The **session transcript** is the documented record of the viewer's session.

- **Feedback** is what is known about the target with regard to the remote viewing task. It provides the gauge against which the viewer's session transcript is judged. Feedback can take many forms: photographs, text, video, sound recordings, personal accounts, actual objects. Feedback should be provided to the viewer after they have completed their session. Feedback is required for remote viewing training/practice.

The Remote Viewing Mindset

The following section contains background information regarding the prevalence of psychic abilities, the capabilities of remote viewing as tested under controlled conditions, and how belief, intention, and expectation play a part in the process; all things to bear in mind as you approach remote viewing.

Remote Viewing Is Possible

Humans, including you, have been able to successfully *describe* predefined targets, *by mental means, blocked from ordinary perception by distance, shielding or time*, whilst adhering to the protocol of blindness.

Here are two examples of first-ever sessions involving two new remote viewers, performed under less-than-ideal conditions in a stuffy room with Manhattan traffic noise.

In the first example, the viewer was given minimal instruction beyond being asked that they calm their mind, bring their attention to a location target and describe it. The target was only referred to by its TRN.

The viewer recorded: Wet / Bubbles / Dark / Round / Sulphur Smell / Pointy / Beige / Craters / Sandy / Crunchy / Water / Polluted? Tar? / Mountains

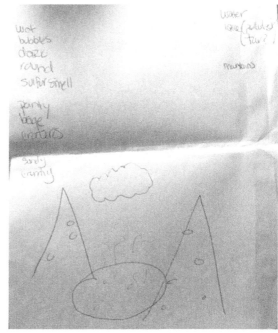

The target was Mount Mayon, an active volcano in the Philippines.

This is a file from the Wikimedia Commons. Author: MERRIJILL A. MEDENILLA

Here is another first attempt; in this example the target is an object, only referred to as 'the object I have brought with me'.

Page 1 of the session captures perception of 'round/empty on the inside'. Perceptions of 'prickly', and 'organic' lead to distracting guesses about kiwis and squishy toy (labelled as 'AOL', which stands for Analytic OverLay; more on this later).

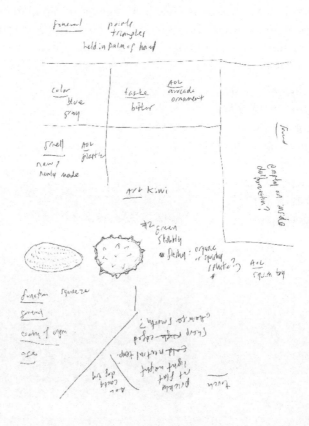

Despite this the viewer succeeds in identifying the basic shape of the object on the second page; 'short curve and long flat' referring to the smaller round portion and the long handle of the target. 'Handle' is named, and there are perceptions that the item is 'industrially made (not organic)', along with the AOLs of 'kitchenware', 'spoon', and 'spatula'.

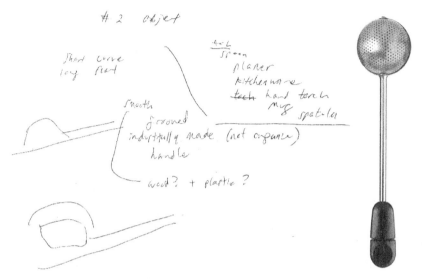

The target was a loose-leaf tea infuser ball.

Psychic Functioning Has Been Well Established

For a broader perspective, a review undertaken in 1995 by Professor Jessica Utts of University of California, Davis and former President of the American Statistical Association, as part of the *AIR Report - Evaluation of Remote Viewing: Research and Applications*, provides a statistical assessment of the output of the United States Government-funded programme. Utts' paper, *An Assessment of the Evidence for Psychic Functioning*, refers to an earlier study conducted by the programme's director of research, Ed May, and his team, which applied a meta-analysis to the experiments undertaken at SRI from 1973 to 1988.[19]

Utts:

> *In 1988 an analysis was made of all the experiments conducted at SRI from 1973 until that time (May et al,*

1988). The analysis was based on all 154 experiments conducted during that era, consisting of over 26,000 individual trials. Of those, almost 20,000 were of the forced choice type and just over a thousand were laboratory remote viewings. There were a total of 227 subjects in all experiments.

The statistical results were so overwhelming that results that extreme or more so would occur only about once in every 10^{20} such instances if chance alone is the explanation (i.e., the p-value was less than 10^{-20}). Obviously some explanation other than chance must be found.

Referring to SAIC, a think-tank organisation similar to SRI, where Ed May continued the research programme from 1991, Utts continues in the document's abstract:

Using the standards applied to any other area of science, it is concluded that psychic functioning has been well established. The statistical results of the studies examined are far beyond what is expected by chance. Arguments that these results could be due to methodological flaws in the experiments are soundly refuted. Effects of similar magnitude to those found in government sponsored research at SRI and SAIC have been replicated at a number of laboratories across the world. Such consistency cannot be readily explained by claims of flaws or fraud.

Regarding replication, in 1982, Hansen, Schlitz and Tart catalogued 28 formal studies that used the SRI outbounder protocol. Not all of them were successful, but many more than by chance.[20]

Utts concludes the paper's abstract with:

There is little benefit to continuing experiments designed to offer proof, since there is little more to be offered to anyone who does not accept the current collection of data.[21]

Further Research Findings

No Lessening of Effect Through Distance

In April 1976, after a number of local outbounder-style experiments had been performed within driving distance of the SRI offices, researchers were confident that the 'phenomenon is not a sensitive function of distance over a range of several kilometres'.[22] By 1979, after the same researchers had conducted several trials over much greater distances (either when experimenters had the chance to travel or when they had the opportunity to make arrangements with colleagues in distant locations) they refined their opinion, stating that 'remote viewing accuracy and reliability were not sensitive functions of either distance or time'.[23]

In 1980, inspired by the published papers from SRI, Marilyn Schlitz and Elmer Gruber ran their own outbounder trials. Whilst Gruber was in Rome, Italy, it was arranged that over the course of 10 consecutive days he would visit a location, selected at random, at a particular time each day, and stay there for 15 minutes. During this specified time each day, Schlitz, in Michigan, in the United States, would focus on her friend's location and record her perceptions. As per the standard outbounder protocol, the results were independently judged. The highly statistical results are recorded in the paper *Transcontinental Remote Viewing*.[24]

To test the range of remote viewing's effectiveness, on 27 April 1973, prior to the NASA Voyager mission, Ingo Swann and Harold Sherman viewed the planet Jupiter. Their responses showed similarities: they both perceived colourful gaseous clouds, high winds, mountains and water. Ingo sketched a ring around the planet and stated, 'Very high in the atmosphere there are crystals... they glitter... maybe like the rings of Saturn'. The results were summarily dismissed as prevailing scientific knowledge precluded the existence of a ring around Jupiter, until the Voyager 1 probe showed just that in 1979.[25]

Swann and Sherman repeated this exercise with the planet Mercury on 11 March 1974, prior to the NASA probe fly-by. Again, their findings 'contained several pieces of data later verified by the Mariner 10 probe that were contrary to the predictions of the astronomers'.[26]

No Lessening of Effect Due to the Size of Target

A series of experiments were conducted at SRI to see if target size made a difference to the quality of the remote viewing.[27] In one a set of various small objects were placed inside 35-mm film canisters (a commonplace item in the days before digital cameras). In another set of experiments, targets were created by shrinking a series of images to fit onto microfilm, smaller than a full stop. Neither size nor lack of light in the sealed canister seemed to diminish the quality of the remote viewing.

In 2011, Debra Katz and Lance Beem ran a project to see if useful information could be gathered via remote viewing for a microscopic biological target - a bacteriophage. Bacteriophages are bacterial viruses that range in length from 24 to 200 nanometers.

Though recruiting scientists for the project proved difficult - many refused to discuss the topic once they found out the source of the data - several were interested enough to commit to review the information. They found, for the best sessions, a high correlation between the data and what is known about the phage. One, a microbiologist, provided the following statement 'At first appearances these data appear to show nothing more than some musings. On further inspection, however, I am convinced that they describe Bacteriophage, and the uses of Bacteriophage. This is my professional opinion as a scientist and a professional and impartial observer'. A further unofficial note was added, 'This is blowing my mind. How is this possible?!...it's scary'.[28]

Remote Viewers Are 'Just Normal People'

Tasked by the CIA with 'the identification of measurable physiological or psychological characteristics of psychic individuals',[29] SRI initiated an extensive series of tests of their remote viewing participants. As Puthoff said: 'We knew more about our people than NASA knew about its astronauts.'[30] The tests were documented in the SRI paper, *Special Orientation Techniques*, from June 1980:

> *...SRI carried out an extensive profiling program on gifted individuals and controls. The tests included a comprehensive medical evaluation, including X-ray*

*scans of the brain, and comprehensive psychological
and neuropsychological profiling.*

A long list of the tests performed is included in the paper.

*The overall result of this testing was that no clear
profile parameters emerged on which an a priori
screening procedure could be based.*

Remote viewers are 'just normal people'.[31] Nothing particularly
unusual about them was found in terms of measurable
physiological or psychological characteristics. The paper continued:

*In contrast to formal testing, however, several years'
observation of remote viewers by SRI researchers has
led to an informal guide based on subjective
evaluation of the personality traits of successful
viewers. This rule-of-thumb guide is based on the
observation that successful remote viewers tend to be
confident, outgoing, adventurous, broadly successful
individuals with some artistic bent.[32]*

In support of this last point, students from New
York's Juilliard School performed above the
general population, achieving a 50% success rate
in ganzfeld studies, double that expected by chance;
and, within that group, music students provided the
highest scores.[33]

Psychic Abilities Are Prevalent

*...the psychic faculties, lie dormant or active in every
individual, and await only that awakening or
arousing... - Edgar Cayce Reading 5752-1*

*EVERY entity has clairvoyant, mystic, psychic powers. -
Edgar Cayce Reading 1500-4*

After over 50 experiments involving more than half a dozen
subjects, Targ and Puthoff noted:

*The principle difference between experienced subjects
and inexperienced volunteers is not that the latter*

never exhibit the faculty, but rather their results are simply less reliable. (This observation suggests the hypothesis that remote viewing may be a latent and widely distributed, though repressed, perceptual ability.)[34]

This hypothesis was supported by mass public experiments arranged by the Mobius organization in the 1980s.[35] It seemed that, like most human capabilities, psychic abilities exist throughout the population in the form of a bell curve distribution; a few are gifted, and some have very little talent, while most of us are somewhere in the middle.

In effect, we are all, to some extent, natural psychics.

SRI researchers used this to their advantage when asked for a demonstration by governmental contract monitors of the project's progress, knowing that any demonstration from a chosen psychic would be open to accusations of fraud. Those asking for a display of a psychic's abilities found themselves being taken through the remote viewing procedure. After the initial shock and protest that they did not know how to do this (in fact, they did not even believe in it), they found themselves producing evidence that implied there was indeed something psychic going on.

Although impossible to prove, a limited distribution of psychic powers to a select few seems, at least to me, an unlikely scenario. It would seem more natural, as with other human abilities, that all of us are somewhere along the bell curve of abilities as postulated by Schwartz, Targ and Puthoff.

An interesting experiment performed by Dean Radin provides evidence of foreknowing, as directly measured from the autonomic nervous system of the body, thus removing any conscious and subjective acknowledgement of the trigger event. Participants were hooked up to devices to measure their skin conductance, then presented with either a benign, tranquil photograph or one designed to evoke an emotive response.

The photograph shown was chosen by a computer just before it was displayed. If a highly charged photograph was selected and shown, the person's body reacted differently than when a tranquil photograph was shown. Nothing surprising in that; however, the differences were measured, in some individuals, up to 5 seconds before the picture was chosen and displayed.[36] These experiments have been replicated several times in different universities. One such replication, by the HeartMath Institute, also included measurements of the heart, which indicated that it plays a role in receiving/feeling intuition. As the researchers stated:

> In short, our findings suggest that intuitive perception is not a discrete function produced by a single part or system of the body alone. Rather, it appears that intuition may in fact be a system-wide process involving at least the heart and brain, together, in the processing and decoding of intuitive information.[37]

A measurable content-specific biological reaction to future events, with some participants reacting more than others, and some not at all, fits the theorized bell curve distribution of psychic abilities.

The whole bell curve, in terms of capability, is likely shifted to a lower spectrum due to science and society's downplaying of psi functioning. This has likely instilled limiting beliefs in the individual, as well as a reticence to admitting an interest in such topics.

However, as we can with any other skill and ability, we can learn and improve and so overcome these beliefs. We may not all be able to produce results at the level of Joe McMoneagle: the talent bell curve is a bell curve after all; but anything we set our mind to with intention, we will make time to learn through exposure to established knowledge and example, and build our own experiences through practice. If we applied this level of conviction to any other human activity, our expectation would be to see an improvement in our abilities.

The goal of this guide is to provide tools for your own personal investigation. For those interested in the prevalence of psychic abilities, there is much to explore online and in books, some starting points being Targ and Puthoff's *Mind-Reach: Scientists Look at Psychic Abilities* (one chapter of which is titled Looking for Gifted Subjects - It Turns Out They're All Gifted!), Targ's *The Reality of ESP - A Physicist's Proof of Psychic Abilities*, and the works of Dean Radin and Daryl Bem.

Belief

What we believe can empower us as well as limit us. If, for example, you believe you cannot perform a good remote viewing session unless you have had a 30-minute meditation, this may limit your ability to perform unless you have the necessary time. If you are told and believe that remote viewing cannot provide text and numbers from a target, this will set up a limiting boundary. Be careful what you accept as beliefs. Question what you read (including this book) and test your assumptions, and those of others, for yourself.

Focus on positive beliefs for yourself: know that psychic abilities are prevalent and remote viewing is possible.

A good belief for the remote viewer to have is that the information the tasker requires is available to you:

The information is already out there; all I have to do is write it down!

Any success at remote viewing should be acknowledged and contemplated. This will strengthen your belief and, as you progress, belief will become knowledge of yourself and your capabilities.

Intention and Expectation

Intention and expectation each play a role in every aspect of our lives, even though we may not be consciously aware of the power of our thoughts.

Remote viewing is intent-driven. The tasker's intent is to gain specific information and the viewer's intent is to supply that information. As intent is a such an important part of the remote viewing process, it is worth stating your own intentions and expectations at the start of your sessions. Your intention is that you will accomplish the task assigned by providing useful and correct information about the target for the tasker.

What do you expect to gain from this exercise? Your expectation is that you will provide the requested information and enjoy a useful session that you will learn from.

Bringing these thoughts to mind before you start your session (during your pre-session cool-down explained below) and remembering during the session that you are performing a task to retrieve information on behalf of the tasker, will focus your intent on the purposeful nature of what you are doing.

Operational and research projects also benefit from a similar team mindset and suffer when it is not in place. Projects tend to be more successful when everyone is committed to the goals of the undertaking and has an expectation of a successful outcome for the project (see May & McMoneagle, *The Possible Role of Intention, Attention, and Expectation in Remote Viewing*, 2004).

An experimenter's own biases, expectations and intentions, whether expressed knowingly and outwardly, or even held subconsciously, are known to influence certain experiments. This effect is so well known that it has a name: the 'observer-expectancy effect' or 'experimenter effect' and has itself been a topic of research.[38] The double-blind protocol may help guard against the effect and is generally adopted in research projects.

'The Remote Viewing Mindset' Section Summary

⊙ Remote viewing is possible; there is a vast store of documented evidence of successful remote viewing, even from first attempts.

⊙ Remote viewers are just normal people. Psychic abilities are latent in all of us, seemingly more widely distributed throughout the population than normally thought.

⊙ There is no lessening of effect due to target size or distance.

⊙ Remote viewing is an intent-driven process. The intentions of the tasker and the viewer form the basis of remote viewing.

⊙ Both belief and expectation of success play a part: *The information is already out there; all you have to do is write it down!*

How to Remote View

Before we look at the mechanics of a remote viewing session, a suggested session format and a procedure for remote viewing, here are the things that remote viewers should be doing during the session, and a few things they should not.

The Job of the Remote Viewer

The remote viewer's job is to

- ⊙ Cool-down - set their intention, and expectation
- ⊙ Recognize and differentiate the artefacts of mental processes of imagination and conjecture
- ⊙ Query all the senses
- ⊙ Write everything down
- ⊙ Record, not analyse
- ⊙ Describe, not name or identify
- ⊙ Sketch

Each of these is an important part of remote viewing.

The 'Cool-down'

An important part of your preparation, prior to performing a session, is getting yourself in a state conducive to remote viewing. This is difficult to achieve if something is playing on your mind. There needs to be a separation between the hustle and bustle and concerns of the day and your remote viewing session. Give yourself some extra time for this separation. This time is referred to as the 'cool-down'.

A meditation practice will help. Yogic and Buddhist texts warn of the distraction of enhanced human abilities (*siddhis* in Sanskrit),[39] including precognition, that appear as a by-product of following a path to enlightenment. Studies with practitioners of these traditions show a link between the number of years of mediation practice and psi abilities.[40]

The ability to calm one's mind and apply focus and attention to the task in hand is an extremely beneficial state of mind to cultivate, and not just for remote viewing. There are many studies citing the wide-ranging benefits of meditation (see Stephan Schwartz' *A Partial Meditation Bibliography 2006-2009*, and the Institute of Noetic Sciences' *Meditation Resources*).

If you are unsure how to meditate, then there are plenty of resources online; Schwartz' *Meditation - The Controlled Psychophysical Self-Regulation Process That Works* is recommended, there are also smart phone apps and online training courses such as *zivaMIND* and *Headspace*.

Many people find listening to calming music to be beneficial to their cool-down process. The Monroe Institute's 'Hemi-Sync' CDs contain sounds and tones designed to enhance relaxation. However, during the remote viewing session itself, you may find that all but very low-level drone-type sounds to be distracting.

The cool-down is a good time to run through your intentions and expectations for the coming session. If something is playing on your mind, the cool-down is the time to set it aside by acknowledging it and asking that it not distract you for the duration of the session. As a remote viewer, you must also clear your mind of any expectations of what the target may be, or even the type of target; nor should there be any desire to name the target. I refer to this clear state of mind as the 'no expectation' state. You need to be a 'blank slate', open to all possibilities. You are not waiting for anything; you are not expecting anything; you are just *being*. You may find it useful to picture this 'no expectation' state as a restful place in your mind, a space of your own with a timeless quality where you can relax. Imagine yourself, for example, in a completely dark or white empty space, or however you might picture 'no expectation' as being a place. You will need to spend some time relaxing in this 'place', so make it comfortable.

The goal of the cool-down is to set the outside world aside for a moment, so that you can turn inward and enter this state of 'no expectation' with a heightened awareness of what you are sensing and feeling, such that when you begin the remote viewing procedure, you will be more aware of how you are responding to your connection to the target.

Each of us will have our own preferred cool-down methods, and requirements in this area, so you will need to find what works for you.

Be careful of establishing the cool-down as an elaborate ritual, which you think you cannot do without, as this will become a barrier to your remote viewing practice. It would be better to define a 'no expectation' state/space that feels comfortable to you, practise your cool-down process, and recognize when you have reached the desired state, so that you can move into it easily when required.

A Cool-down Approach

One approach to practising this is to slowly and systematically bring your attention to each area of your body in turn and ask that it be calm and relaxed. With your eyes closed and feet on the floor (or lying down), focus on your breathing and take several slow, relaxed deep breaths. Now breathe regularly and imagine each part of the body releasing tension, and feel it relax. Start with your head. Bring your attention to your eyes, and ask that they relax, and enjoy the sense of relaxation. Then bring your attention to your eyelids and ask that they relax. Enjoy them relaxing.

Follow the same procedure with your cheeks, mouth, jaw and forehead. Bring your attention to each area and enjoy the relaxation of each. This will create a sense of heaviness in your head. Take a moment to enjoy this feeling.

Allow this heavy, relaxed feeling to flow from your head through your shoulders and down your arms, relaxing these areas as it goes, and towards your hands and fingers. Then allow the relaxing feeling to flow through your body towards your legs, and down to your ankles and toes. Along the way, stop at each area, give it some attention and enjoy a sense of relaxation. By the time you have done this, you should feel extremely relaxed, in a deep state of 'no expectation'.

The Relaxation Response

If you think the process described above is a bit involved, the technique outlined in the book *The Relaxation Response* is a simple and quick way to get centred. Its author, Herbert Benson, MD, investigated meditation in the 1970s and found that it had huge benefits to health in general, particularly in helping people deal with stress. Benson and his team devised a simple method: in a comfortable position, relax with your eyes closed and bring your attention to your breathing. Take in a full breath and, on the outbreath, internally say to yourself a single word. This can be any word you like, but a simple, one-syllable word that has some meaning to you, such as 'one' or 'calm' or 'love', would be better. Bringing some sense of what your chosen word means to you, by invoking a memory that captures the emotion of the word, will underscore its meaning for you. For example, if your word is 'love', you could think of something or someone you love, such as your spouse, child or pet.

Maintain a passive attitude when distracting thoughts arise, as they will; do not engage them, calmly acknowledge them and return to saying your word on the outbreath. Tell yourself that there is plenty of time to fuss and worry later; for now, you just want to focus on this exercise. With practice, its effects will come to you more readily. To get the full effect, it is meant to be practised twice a day for 20 minutes.

As this method is so simple and does not require anything more than your intent and a passive attitude (this was found to be the most important aspect), you can do it anywhere. Although a comfortable position may help, you can even do it on your commute or just when you have a few spare moments. Focusing on your breathing and your chosen word to calm your mind, instead of getting frustrated on public transport or sitting in traffic, will do your heart, mind and body good, as well as prepare you for your remote viewing practice.

HeartMath Institute

The method set out in *The Relaxation Response* is similar to that promoted by the HeartMath Institute. This organization has much to offer in the way of meditation exercises and research. They have two systems that provide biofeedback reinforcement for your meditation practice: an iPhone application that works in conjunction with a small clip, and a small self-contained unit called the 'emWave2'. Both devices measure heart rate variability, a 'non-invasive measure of autonomic nervous-system function and an indicator of neurocardiac fitness'.[41]

Psychic Impressions

Psychic impressions are often very subtle, and our perception of them can seem like a distant memory, a mere hint of a feeling, or just a 'knowing'; you may not know quite why, but you will find yourself writing something down.

Think of yourself as the receiver, one part of a remote viewing *system* that is accessing and capturing information. For the weak signal of these subtle impressions to register amidst the noise of our mind chatter, you need to be in a relaxed, receptive and open state of awareness - the 'no expectation' state, attuned to the inner world of what you are feeling and sensing.

Remote Viewing Is Not Analysis

In the conclusions to their paper of March 1976, *A Perceptual Channel for Information Transfer Over Kilometer Distances*, Targ and Puthoff stated:

> *Most of the correct information that subjects relate is of a nonanalytical nature pertaining to shape, form, color, and material rather than to function or name. (This aspect suggests a hypothesis that information transmission under conditions of sensory shielding may be mediated primarily by the brain's right hemisphere).*[42]

This statement underscores a core tenet of remote viewing's procedural approach, that is, towards description and away from the products of analysis: classification and naming.

Psychic impressions do not come as a function of analysis. You will not work out the answer with reasoning; in fact, analytical thoughts will hinder the process of recording what you are sensing and feeling. Remote viewing is a right-brain activity and requires a meditative state of mind, like losing yourself in something creative, such as painting, or the state achieved when playing a musical instrument; intently focused, yet relaxed. You have likely had the experience of being so engrossed in an activity that, upon reflection, it seemed you were in some timeless state. The terms 'flow state' and 'the zone' are sometimes used to describe this state when related to creative and athletic activities. This is the mental state required. Help maintain this state by not analysing as you go. Do not try and work out what the target is. Psychic impressions are to be received without judgement. Judgement requires analysis. The remote viewer's job is to <u>record their impression of the target, not analyse</u>. Leave any preconceptions behind. Be open to all possibilities.

If It's Too Good to Be True...

For most of us, psychic impressions are fleeting, dim, blurred.

If you do have the impression of a stable, clear and vivid image, or feel you can identify the target, the chances are that it is your imagination presenting you with a pleasant image. Write it down, but do not build on it.

You are unlikely to get the big picture in one shot; instead, you'll probably receive a bit of information here and a bit there, pieces that may not appear to make sense together, as they come piecemeal from the individual senses, especially in the early stages of the session. If the information you are perceiving does seem out of place and does not tell a coherent story, it is not necessarily wrong; in fact, it could well be a sign that you are on the right track.

If it seems your perceptions are fitting together too well this may be a sign that a part of you has created a model of what it believes the target to be, and your imagination is happily providing more information to match this model. Going down this road further supports and builds your imaginary model and makes it harder for you to recognise it for what it is, and move away from it. Unfortunately, it is difficult to know when this is happening, but you need to guard against it by doing what you can to ensure the information you perceive is coming through your psychic channels.

Your awareness of the target should build from a base of sensory impressions - sounds, smells, colours, textures, shapes - received by querying each of your senses independently, followed by probing for more complex information.

Analytic Overlay

Being able to discern between the subtle psychic signal, the random noise of our minds and the artefacts produced from analytical processes, such as conjecture, is the skill of the remote viewer. As mentioned above, it is highly likely that, in the early stages of your session, any fixed, clear images and nouns that come to mind are unlikely to be direct psychic perceptions.

These could simply be random thoughts that have appeared as your relaxed mind has an opportunity to present you with some images that it feels are important for you to see at this moment.

It is, however, more likely that they are products of the left brain, the analytical mind, wanting to help by providing its best guess based on analysis, memory or imagination triggered by a limited amount of psychic information. The results, that is, what appears in your consciousness, are known as 'analytic overlay'; an overlay of the analytical thought processes on top of the psychic signal. 'AOL' for short.

Accepting, that is, acknowledging and recording, the artefacts of analytical processes as psychic perception could lead to the generation of further potentially incorrect information. Let's say you received the following impressions: blue, warm, yellow and sandy, and then an image of a beach scene came to mind: a picturesque postcard image of people sunbathing and swimming in the sea.

If the *beach scene* was accepted and written down as psychic perception, it would be very difficult to move away from this image - your analytical mind will happily provide yet more 'evidence' that it is a beach scene. In fact, if given a chance, it will embellish any 'perception' to provide a very convincing description of some figment of your imagination. It will build a story where all the pieces fit together, all without any psychic functioning. You'll think you've had a great session, but you will be disappointed.

The target may be a beach scene, but it may not; it could be a desert or a construction site.

Accepting the image will embolden the thought processes that produced it, and could lead you down a path that is incorrect.

Instead, if you recognized and classified the *beach scene* image as AOL, perhaps because it seemed like a memory or because the image was just too clear and vivid, you would be more likely to be able to clear it from your mind, allowing new psychic perceptions to be received, unhindered by the functions of the left brain. You need to leave your options open, keeping the door open to allow real psychic information to be perceived.

Recording Analytic Overlay

Information that is considered to be AOL should be acknowledged by being written down, but separately from your psychic perceptions, to allow you to make a distinction between the two.

There are a number of conventions for recording AOL separately from your psychic perceptions. The easiest is to format each page, before you start using it, by drawing a vertical line an inch or so from the right side of your paper and labelling the top of this column 'AOL'. This splits the page into two, the smaller column to the right to record AOL, and the larger portion to the left for everything else. This is shown in the 'Session Format' section and the example sessions below.

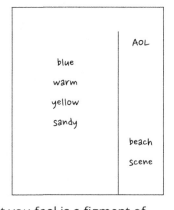

Anything suspected of being AOL should be placed in this separate area, but in line with the flow of the rest of the information. To do this, move your pen to the AOL column on the right side of the page, write down the noun or the text you feel is a figment of your memory or imagination, and take a break. Taking a break means moving your awareness away from the target. Ensure you do this. Put your pen down. Focus on your breathing, clear your mind, and rest in your comfortable 'no expectation' state/place in your mind. When ready, when you feel the image or thought you've classified as AOL has dissipated, and you can move on without its interference, pick up your pen and, on the line below, move back to the left side of the page to continue recording your next perception. This retains the order in which the information was recorded. This is explained further in the 'A Procedure for Remote Viewing' section.

Use All Your Senses!

Although more technically correct, the terms *anomalous perception, anomalous cognition* and *remote sensing* have not caught on publicly, with *remote viewing* remaining prevalent. Originally coined by Swann during experiments made at the American Society for Psychical Research (ASPR) in the early 1970's, 'remote viewing' was adopted by the SRI programme to distinguish it from the baggage associated with the more commonly used terms. Despite the name, all senses are available, and your remote viewing procedure should make a point of querying each of them.

The hearing, olfactory (sense of smell) and gustatory (taste) senses are often forgotten but can supply valuable information.

You can psychically taste objects to get information (do not worry, you are not physically putting things in your mouth); for example, woody or metallic tastes can give an indication of the types of materials at the target.

Ambient sound can give an impression of whether the target is inside or out and offer clues to any type of activity that is taking place.

We perceive the world through more than the traditional five physical senses. We sense balance, movement and pressure.

We also feel emotions, in ourselves and in others. Our subjective feelings about the target can provide pertinent information. Put yourself in the presence of the target ('I am at the target') and become aware of what you are feeling and record it. Feeling alone, as if you are in a desolate area, or being too high up and a bit scared, or feeling comfortable and happy, as if in an idyllic setting, can help towards describing the target.

The key to remote viewing is being aware of what you are feeling and sensing in your inner world when you have the remote viewing target as the focus of your attention. Your remote viewing session is a record of your experience of the target.

Write Everything Down!

Write everything down! This includes the AOLs and all the things that do not make sense. There is nothing worse than looking at the target feedback after the session and saying, 'I knew that, but didn't write it down!' If it is not written down, it doesn't count.

 The remote viewer's job is to <u>record, not analyse</u>.

If you start filtering out information - because it sounds 'funny' and does not fit with the image you are building of the target - then you are not recording; you are in left-brain mode, analysing and making judgements, trying to work out what the target is. This is not your job; nor are you in a position to say what fits and what does not, as you do not know what the target is.

It is the correct, yet incongruous and unusual, pieces of information that are the most rewarding as they show a clear connection to the target.

Keep your language at the level of basic, descriptive words, especially at the start of your session. Structuring sentences, searching for just the right word and remembering how to spell are all analytical activities that should be minimized during your session. When remote viewing, just write the information down; after the session, you can write a summary in properly constructed sentences, with correct spelling and grammar.

 <u>Describe, not name</u>. Your aim is *not* to identify, classify or name, but to record your experience of the target.

As soon as you think you 'know' what the target is and you put a name to it, not only are you very likely to be wrong, but your analytical mind will now make it very difficult for psychic information to present itself, as part of you will want to reinforce the model it is building. Throughout the process, you need to remain open to new information.

Minimize your use of nouns and instead focus on adjectives to describe textures, colours, shapes, sounds, tastes and smells. As an example, it would be better to describe the attributes of a something you felt to be a table, e.g., as a 'flat, smooth, horizontal plane, raised off the ground, that is hard, brown, woody and rectangular', than to simply write 'coffee table'. The tasker's idea of a coffee table may be very different from yours; also, it may not be a coffee table at all, but something that has the same characteristics. (If you do get the impression of a coffee table, it should be noted in the AOL column. Classifying 'coffee table' as AOL will convey to the tasker/analyst looking at your session that aspects of the target reminded you of a coffee table.)

Committing your perceptions to paper is an acknowledgement and acceptance of them and doing so allows for new information to be received. This may sound unusual, but if you do not write them down, they will keep rattling around inside your head and your left brain will build on them. Your analytical mind desperately wants to be involved in this process – don't give it the opportunity.

Sketching Is Essential

Your remote viewing sketches are not art competition entries or an exercise in technical drawing; the purpose of sketching in remote viewing is to strengthen your connection with the target to be able to gain more information about it. As sketching is more of a creative and less of an analytical process than our use of language, it can bypass some of the obstacles of left-brain analysis.

You are not converting what you are perceiving into words; in fact, you do not need to consciously know what you are sketching, or even know what you have sketched after you have sketched it.

This rough sketch of the back of an ornamental porcelain hippopotamus made little sense to the viewer's conscious mind; however, I knew the viewer was on target, as I knew what the target was (the viewer also recorded green/smooth/ridged, which were all correct).

Interestingly, the view captured is from the viewpoint of how I had placed the object down on the viewer's desk for feedback.

Even if you do not 'know' what to sketch, focus your intent on the target, place your pen on the paper, give your arm a bit of a 'push' and allow it to doodle on its own. You'll be surprised. Your subconscious knows more about the target than you do and will guide you. Try to *feel* the outline of the target as you sketch. You may find that your pen knows where to go next, so allow it to do what feels right.

Several sketches should be made, both to refine your initial view and to capture the target from different angles.

Sketches can lead to more information becoming available. Trace over the lines you have made with the expectation of receiving more information. This may reveal texture and colour, along with other perceptions from that particular part of the target.

You can also use this process to explore the space inside your sketch: is it uniform, or are there different textures, colours or areas inside?

What is near the target? We will look at this in more detail later; the probing method can be used to explore the area around the target, providing information to establish the setting or context of the target.

'The Job of the Remote Viewer' Section Summary

Left brain/right brain - These terms are a useful generalization for referring to thinking modes: the left-brain mode being the logical, analytical side, used for language and mathematics; and the right-brain mode as the creative side, such as in producing and appreciating art and music. Remote viewing is more a function of the right-brain mode and seems to suffer from interference from left-brain mode thinking.

- ⊙ Find a comfortable meditative 'no expectation' state/space of your own and practise relaxing there.

- ⊙ Prior to remote viewing, run through your cool-down process: set aside any concerns playing on your mind, set your intention and expectation of success and, most importantly, clear any preconceptions of the target from your mind.

- ⊙ Aim to describe your experience of the target, not name it.

- ⊙ Use all your senses.

- ⊙ Write everything down, if it's not written down, it doesn't count! Record, don't analyse.

- ⊙ Use short descriptive words; do not worry about forming full sentences and correct spelling.

- ⊙ Watch out for AOL, normally identifiable by the use of nouns, distinct images, or when the pieces just seem to be fitting together too well. Record, but as 'AOL', and take a break to clear your mind before continuing.

- ⊙ Use sketching as a way to engage with the target. Allow yourself to freely sketch, with your intent focused on gaining information.

The Mechanics of a Remote Viewing Session

This section explains the use and function of the target reference number, how a remote viewing session is initiated, and a suggested format for recording the session.

The remote viewing process starts with the tasker formulating their request for information into a task. To satisfy the protocol of viewer blindness, the target is only identified, and communicated to the viewer, by what is known as a 'coordinate' or target reference number.

The Coordinate or Target Reference Number

A target reference number (TRN) is a short numeric or alphanumeric code that represents the intent of the tasker in such a way that it hides the actual description of the task from the viewer.

The tasker assigns the TRN as part of setting up the task. It is often a code based on the date on which the task was set or assigned; for example, the tasker may use a YYMMDD format giving a numeric code such as '180831'. However, it does not have to use the date, it could be any series of numbers, or numbers and letters. The combination of letters and even some numbers can be interpreted as spelling out words (for example '130Y' could be read as 'BOY'), the tasker should ensure this is not the case with their TRN as this could influence the viewer. To minimise this possibility many taskers do not use letters. A common convention is to use two sets of four random numbers, e.g., 5656 / 7865.

As an example, say the tasker thinks the London Eye would make a good practise target and finds a suitable photograph as the feedback. Once the task has been defined, it is associated to the TRN.

Task 5656/7865

'London Eye' - describe from the point of view of the
photograph, at the time the photograph was taken.

Note, the viewer would not see the task until after the session.

You can think of the TRN as a street address to a building in a town you have never been to. As the viewer, you are blind to the target; you do not know what type of structure it is or what is inside, but you have the address.

Viewers who have been through CRV training will expect a TRN; however, it is not actually needed at all. You can be assigned a target by being told by the tasker, 'I have a target for you', while you can refer to a target by saying to yourself, 'Target - what do I perceive?', as long as your intention is fixed on the target you have been assigned.

However, the TRN does make it easier to talk about and reference specific targets.

A Brief History of the Target Reference Number

The introduction and use of the TRN is an interesting story in the history of remote viewing. Initial experiments at SRI used a person, known as an 'outbounder', who would be sent to an undisclosed location, to act as a beacon for the remote viewer to home in on. The task presented to the viewer would be along the lines of, 'Describe where Hal Puthoff is now'. Although practical for research, this type of targeting would be of little benefit to operational remote viewing, in particular for the espionage purposes SRI's initial client would have been interested in.

As Swann tells it, during his initial stay in California working with SRI he was relaxing in the pool of his rented apartment complex,
 enjoying a bottle of scotch, contemplating the targeting issue, when he heard a voice say, 'Try coordinates', meaning longitude and latitude coordinates.[43]

Initially sceptical, as they saw no explanation of how it could possibly work, Puthoff and Targ finally agreed to at least trying the

46

new method, and a series of experiments were conducted that used coordinates (with the implied task of, 'Describe what is at geographic coordinates...'). As these experiments were successful, this method of target identification by coordinates was implemented.

However, the use of geographic coordinates has several issues. One criticism is that 'the viewer could have memorized the world's coordinate grid' and used their knowledge of it to describe the location. In fact, ex-military remote viewer Paul H. Smith has stated that the military viewers became so familiar with the regions associated with particular geographic coordinates, that it did become a hindrance to the process, as it front-loaded them with an expectation that the target was in a particular region.

The coordinate convention was also not practical for targets other than locations; geographical coordinates cannot reference an object, person or an event.

Through further experimentation, however, it became apparent that the numbers actually represented the intent of the tasker for information, and that any numbers or code could be applied to any kind of task and target.

Session Format

As this is guide is a procedure for *natural* remote viewing, you are free to use your own format to record your session, as long as you followed the guidance in the previous sections; that is, everything is written down, AOL is differentiated from your other perceptions, and sketches are made.

Here, however, is an example of a suggested format, showing the layout and information you should record.

Before commencing your remote viewing session, note down the administrative information in the top right: Documenting your name, the date, the time and the place you undertook the session will make it a more formal exercise, and will help you and anyone looking at your sessions in the future.

Preformat the page with the 'AOL' column by drawing a line an inch or so from the right edge of the page before starting and labelling the top of it 'AOL'.

```
                                              Your name

                                              Your location

                                                     Date

                                                     Time

                                  |             AOL
 - - - - - - - - - - - - - - - - -  - - - - - - - - -
```

If you use more than one piece of paper (and don't feel you need to cram everything on to one page – don't restrict yourself), just number each page in the top right-hand corner so they can be kept in order and draw in the AOL column before you start each new page.

```
                                              Jon N.

                                              Brooklyn, NY

                                              31 August 2018

                                                     17:00

  5656/7865                  |             AOL


  Blue, orange
  Dusty
  Grey


  Metallic
```

Thin	Eiffel Tower
Framework	
Hard	
curved	Bicycle wheel
Round	
White	
Tall	
Flat	People visiting
Smooth	
water	
End 17:15	

Note that the TRN is written at the beginning of the session. Perceived information is recorded on the left side of the page, primarily as adjectives - remember: describe, not name. Anything in which you feel your own analytical processes (naming, analysis and conjecture) may have played a part should be recorded on the right side of the page in the 'AOL' column.

The session is formally closed by writing 'End' and recording the time.

A summary should be written after the session. The summary presents the information in structured sentences and in a logical manner, making it easier for anyone reviewing your session to understand what you have found.

P. 2

Summary

Target appears to be a structure. It is tall, round and made of a hard, metallic material in a framework that reminded me of the Eiffel Tower or a bicycle wheel.

colours are blue, orange, white and grey.

Structure appears to be set on its own in a flat area.

Water is present.

People visit this place.

At the start of this process, you would only have been informed of the TRN, and no other information. The TRN would have been provided to you in a simple message:

The target is 5656/7865.

You, the viewer, are blind to the target.

Along with the task, here is an example of the type of feedback that you should receive after your session:

Feedback 5656/7865

From Wikipedia, the free encyclopedia

The London Eye is a giant Ferris wheel on the South Bank of the River Thames in London.

The structure is 443 feet (135 m) tall and the wheel has a diameter of 394 feet (120 m). When it opened to the public in 2000 it was the world's tallest Ferris wheel. Its height was surpassed by the 525-foot (160 m) Star of Nanchang in 2006, the 541-foot (165 m) Singapore Flyer in 2008, and the 550-foot (167.6 m) High Roller (Las Vegas) in 2014. Supported by an A-frame on one side only, unlike the taller Nanchang and Singapore wheels, the Eye is described by its operators as "the world's tallest cantilevered observation wheel".

It is Europe's tallest Ferris wheel, and offered the highest public viewing point in London until it was superseded by the 804-foot (245 m) high observation deck on the 72nd floor of The Shard, which opened to the public on 1 February 2013. It is the most popular paid tourist attraction in the United Kingdom with over 3.75 million visitors annually, and has made many appearances in popular culture.

The rim of the Eye is supported by tensioned steel cables and resembles a huge spoked bicycle wheel.

A Procedure for Remote Viewing

The following procedure is derived from Skip Atwater's set of behaviours for remote viewing as described in the 'Remote-Viewing Training and Operations' chapter of his book, *Captain of My Ship, Master of My Soul*.

The behaviours form an iterative procedure of five steps: relax, prompt, listen, become aware and record.

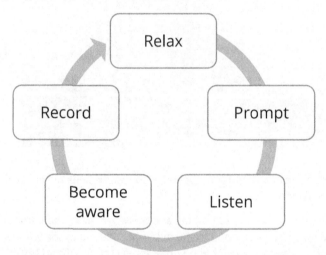

In essence, the procedure is a question ('prompt') and answer ('become aware') dialogue between you and the rest of the system involved in supplying the information, with steps for you to record ('record') the answer (your perceptions), and to reset ('relax') before moving onto your next question. This procedure is repeated in order to query each of your senses and ask each of your questions independently, until you feel you have learned all you can about the target to meet the needs of the task, and answer the tasker's questions.

Each of the steps is described below. This is followed by a walk-through exercise to put the procedure in the context of a remote viewing session.

1. Relax

It sounds simple, but relaxing is something that many of us have forgotten how to do effectively. It is, however, the key to successful remote viewing.

The goal is to reach a state of 'no expectation': your mind should be clear of any expectation of what the target might be, becoming a 'blank slate', open to all possibilities. You are neither waiting for anything nor expecting anything; you are just in a state of *beingness*.

You may already have a technique to get yourself centred and relaxed; if not, here are a few approaches to try out. Test each and discard them if they do not feel right for you:

- ⊙ With your feet on the floor, take several slow, deep breaths, and bring a calming image to  mind, perhaps a place, real or imaginary, where you feel relaxed. Then let the image go, and just relax.

- ⊙ Imagine, think or feel you have no head, and that you are breathing in and out of your body (not through your mouth). This should create a sense of open space around you.

- ⊙ Imagine, with each outbreath you are taking, a step down a staircase and, with each imagined step, you are becoming more relaxed and calm.

While these methods may seem disconcerting at first, their goal is to quickly calm your mind, minimize the sense of your physical surroundings, and heighten the sense of your inner world. You may feel a lightness of your awareness, and its ability to move about on its own, unencumbered by the physical body.

If they are not meeting this goal and becoming a distraction, then just focus on your breathing and the relaxation of your body.

When you feel ready, move onto the next step...

2. Prompt

In the state of 'no expectation', bring your awareness to the target by saying and thinking of the target coordinate, (or simply 'target', if there is no TRN). In doing so, you are directing your intention and making a connection to the target.

Command yourself clearly and specifically. Tell yourself, *you are really in the presence of the target.* You are not only engaging yourself in this process, but also the other parts of your remote viewing system involved in supplying the information. Let this system know you *mean business* and have an expectation of correct information being supplied in response to your query.

The first time through the procedure, you are looking to capture your initial impressions of the target. On subsequent iterations, this step is used to query each of your senses individually and ask for specific information.

Remote viewing is an intent-driven process. Focus your intention on a specific sense or the specific information you are looking for at each prompt. Do this by bringing your awareness to the target by thinking of the TRN and stating your question, e.g., '5656 7865, what can I smell?'. You can reinforce the query by bringing your awareness to the particular part of the body involved in experiencing that sense. If you feel it helps, you can also make the physical motion involved with that sense, e.g., sniff the air, reach out your hand as if feeling the texture, etc.

3. Listen

Now move from the state of 'no expectation' to a state of open 'expectation' - you have asked a question and now expect an answer.

There are two approaches to the length of time you should stay 'listening' after the 'prompt' stage: long and short. Try waiting for a little while - seconds, not minutes - and see what appears to your awareness. Here, you are expecting something specific to make itself known to your conscious awareness; if it does then you have moved on to the 'become aware' step.

The Quick Listen/Awareness/Record Combination

As this may not be the case, another approach is to assume that psychic information is already available to your subconscious, and *all you need to do is write it down*. This means making yourself write something down that you are not fully consciously aware of, skipping the 'become aware' step.

You are probably thinking, 'How can I write something down if I don't know what to write down?'. Take the approach that you do know the answer, or at least your subconscious does. *The information is already out there, all you need to do is write it down.* If you *had to* write to something, what would you write? The first thing that comes to you, write it down!

The advantage of the second, quick approach is that it gives the conscious level of the mind very little chance to embellish with imagination, or transform via memory - you are writing without thinking.

4. Become Aware

Still in a relaxed, open state, become aware of a sense, perhaps a feeling, a colour or a smell - some perception. You may sense a series of impressions all at once; for example, several colours may come to mind.

If nothing comes to mind, stay calm and do not force it, as your analytical mind will make something up. Stay relaxed and open, and then move onto your next prompt. You can always query the same sense or ask the same question later.

It is important not to judge or analyse the received perception, but to immediately move to the 'record' step.

5. Record

Objectify - get it out! Write it down, say it out loud.

Keep your responses at the level of single words or short phrases, especially when describing your sensory experience of the target. Use short, basic words, such as 'cold', 'hard', 'flat' or 'red', simple words that are unambiguous. Do not go to the effort of crafting full sentences, or ensuring your spelling and grammar are correct - just get the words down on paper. You may find that, during the session, your spelling and handwriting are not at their best. This is a sign that the analytical part of your brain, the part that can spell, is less engaged. This is good, so do not worry about it during the session. If you start thinking about how to spell a word, you will fire up the analytical mind. (After the remote viewing session, when you can safely engage your analytical thinking, you can craft a summary written with as much detail as you like, involving full sentences with correct grammar and spelling.)

Write everything down! Saying 'I knew that!', after you have seen the feedback, doesn't count.

If you feel the need to use nouns or describe complex concepts, or you have the image of a clear picture in your mind, or you feel conjecture played a part in what you're perceiving, take this as an indication that the analytical mind is at work - potential AOL. These should be recorded as such. On your paper, move your pen to the line below, and directly sideways to the AOL column on the right side of the page and write them down. Then, immediately take a break by putting your pen down and clearing your mind by moving your awareness onto something other than the target, such as your breath; in effect, spend some extra time at the 'relax' step. Pick up your pen and return to the target with the next prompt. Write the next perception you receive on the left side of the page, but directly below the AOL entry. This retains the order in which the information was perceived and recorded.

This completes the five steps.

Repeat the Steps

Now repeat the steps. Get yourself into the relaxed, 'no expectation' state. Be conscious of clearing your mind before moving onto your next prompt. Your next perception should come from psychic sources and not be a product of analysis of previously received information. Rather, try and clear your mind of whatever has been received and recorded up to this point. The timing of this may take a little practise; you don't want to stop and hinder the flow of psychic information, but you also don't want to encourage the analytical mind by allowing it a chance to start making things up.

Continue looping through the steps until you have queried each of your senses and all the questions that you feel are relevant to the target.

Prompts

In real life, we initially notice an object's or location's most discerning features. Do not hamper this natural function by initiating your first contact with the target focused on one particular sense. Instead, just bring your attention to the target in a relaxed, open state of mind and capture any feelings or impressions.

After this, run through each of your senses in turn. I don't believe the order in which they are queried is important, just they are all queried. However, you may feel more comfortable testing each in a particular order.

After querying your senses, get a sense of space and a feel of the dimensions of the target; capture these as words to start with, for example, 'wide, tall, open', and make a sketch when you feel the need to. Trace over sketches with the intent of feeling and sensing for more information.

Then, prompt for your subjective feelings about the target by bringing your attention to it and asking, 'How do I feel?'.

Follow this with a range of your own questions that you feel fit the target (I've listed my suggestions below).

This is a suggested order. Do not reject anything that does not arrive in this sequence, for example you may feel a sense of the age of the target before any physical sense perceptions, or feel the need to sketch early in the process. This is all fine. Again, do not analyse; just record.

There will be information about the target that you will not have a question/prompt for, so you also need to have open prompts where you just spend time with your awareness at the target and allow any perceptions to come to you. Do this several times, at least at the beginning, and at the end of your session.

Prompts should be clear and specific, focusing on querying a sense or requesting particular information. They are best stated as open questions, open to any response. Forced choice questions that presuppose information, such as 'How many people are present?', which assumes that people are there, will encourage analytical thinking to provide an 'answer' - you will make something up. Our natural tendency is to answer questions using our analytical capabilities, even though we do not know what the answers are, we will still guess at something based on what little we think we know. This desire needs to be replaced with an engagement with the remote viewing process: either resting in the state of 'no expectation' or engaged in connecting with the target and gaining information from it.

Throughout the process use the 'prompt' step to reaffirm your intent and bring the purposefulness of what you are doing to mind. Remember that you are finding useful information for the tasker. Reconnect and strengthen your connection to the target by restating 'target' or the TRN as you feel necessary, e.g. '5656 7865 - What can I hear?'.

Imagine, think, and feel you are really in the presence of the target.

Suggested prompts:
I've used the first-person pronoun, 'I', in these, but some self-hypnosis guides and self-talk procedures recommended the use of the second-person, so you may wish to experiment with 'you'.

- What can I hear?
- What can I taste?
- What can I smell?
- What texture can I feel?
- What is the temperature?
- What can I see?
- What colours are present (and what are the qualities of colours)?

- ⊙ What sense of space is there at the target? (Are there any horizontal, vertical or diagonal spatial elements?)
- ⊙ What shapes are there? (Make a sketch and explore the space.)
- ⊙ What is the most representative view of this target? (Make another sketch.)
- ⊙ How do I feel about the target?
- ⊙ Get a sense of the age of the target: is it old or new?
- ⊙ What distinctive or unusual features does the target have?
- ⊙ What significance, purpose or use does the target have?
- ⊙ What does the tasker want to know about the target?
- ⊙ Is there anything else I need to know about the target that would be useful for the tasker?

For all types of targets, ask questions that you sense are necessary, that you feel need to be asked. You will likely be requesting information required by the task.

If you do not become aware of any perceptions after the 'prompt' step, then remain relaxed and move onto your next question. You can always repeat the question or query the same sense again later in the session.

Object Target

If you know from front-loading, or sense during the session that the target is an object, prompt yourself with specific questions that would be relevant to it.

- Gauge its size: does the item fit in my hand?
- I have the object in my hand, what does it feel like? (Get a feel for its size, weight, texture and temperature).
- How large is the item compared to me? (Imagine yourself standing next the object, are you looking up at it?)
- Does it have any moving parts?
- Get a sense of country or region of origin
- Who made it?
- Who owns it?
- What is the object's setting or context?

As a general open question, that may or may not produce an answer: Does the object have a story that is relevant to the tasker's query?

Location Target

If you know the target is a location...

- Sense the environment, smell the air, listen – am I inside or outside?
- Sense whether people are present and if so, what are they doing and what is their mood?

Try and ascertain if the target is a structure. If so...

- What materials do I feel?
- Is it natural or man-made?
- Get a sense of the size of the structure (compared to a person).
- Does it have an inside?

What is the target's setting?

- ⊙ I am standing at the target location; what do I feel under my feet?
- ⊙ What is the temperature at the location?
- ⊙ What are the weather conditions?
- ⊙ What features (textures, colours) does the location around the target have?
- ⊙ What other elements (natural or man-made) are located around the target?
- ⊙ In which country or region is the location?

Person Target

If you know, or sense, that the target is a person, then imagine yourself in their presence, at the time they are their most representative self or performing the function they are best known for, and...

- ⊙ Observe the person: what are they doing?
- ⊙ What are these other people doing?
- ⊙ What style of clothing is the person wearing?
- ⊙ How tall is the person compared to me? (Imagine standing next them)
- ⊙ Engage the person: ask them to show you what they do.
- ⊙ What is the person's temperament?
- ⊙ Make a sketch of their face, with the intent of capturing their recognizable features.
- ⊙ Describe the location.
- ⊙ Are other people here with me?
- ⊙ What is the person doing currently?
- ⊙ What is their current location?

Event Target

If you sense movement or some activity at the target, then try and ascertain the purpose of the activity; who is involved, what they are doing and why. Are people involved, as participants or spectators? What emotions are there from those present? What are your feelings?

Using the ability to move around the target (described later), it may be possible to move to another time and perceive changes over the course of the event and the outcome.

Take a Break

Left-brain analytical processes will supply sensations and feelings that support their own theory of what is being perceived. You can reduce this natural function by re-entering the meditative state by running through a mini cool-down process. Do this whenever you feel your responses are perhaps the result of conjecture and imagination, or you simply need a break from the psychic process. A break from the process and a regaining of the 'no expectation' state will more likely enable discernment between random thoughts, AOL and true psychic perceptions.

To effectively take a break, you should put your pen down and sit back. Make a point of disengaging from the target by moving your awareness towards something other than the target, such as your breathing. Clear your mind and find the 'no expectation' state/place in your mind and relax there.

The End

Your session should be formally closed by writing 'End' and noting the time. Consciously detach from the target by engaging in some other activity.

Example Session

Below is an example session followed by a walk-through exercise of the procedure in the context of a remote viewing session.

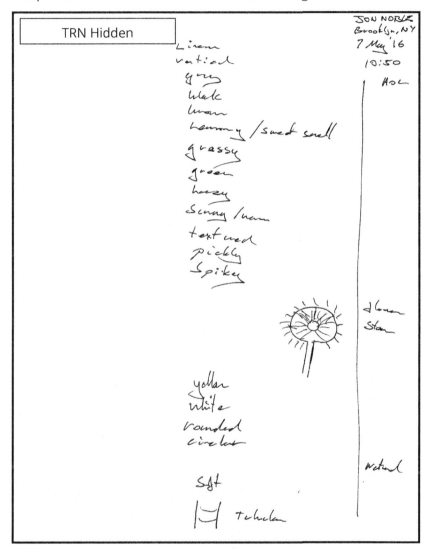

Linear / Vertical / Grey / black / Brown / Lemony / Sweet Smell / Grassy / Green / Hazy / Sunny / Warm / Textured / Prickly / Spikey / AOL Flower Stem / Yellow / White / Rounded / Circular / AOL Natural / Soft / Tubular

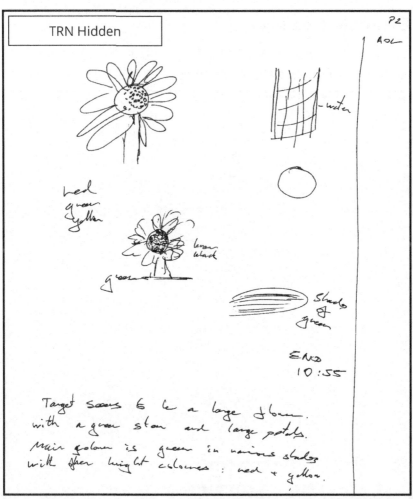

Water / Red / Green / Yellow / Brown / Black / Green / Shades of green

Target seems to be a large flower, with a green stem and large petals. Main colour is green in various shades with other bright colours: red and yellow.

Session Walk-through Exercise

Now it's your turn.

To put the procedure described above into the context of a remote viewing session, you are going to perform a remote viewing exercise.

The target's TRN is **RVPG Y171.**

Front-loading for this target is that it is a location on earth.

You may want to review the previous sections to get into the remote viewing mindset and remind yourself of the job of the remote viewer. Here is a recap of some of the keys points:

- ⊙ Prior to remote viewing, run through your cool-down process: set aside any concerns playing on your mind, set your intention and expectation of success and, most importantly, clear any preconceptions of the target from your mind.
- ⊙ Aim to describe your experience of the target, not name it.
- ⊙ Use all your senses.
- ⊙ Write everything down: if it is not written down, it does not count! Record, don't analyse.
- ⊙ Use short descriptive words; don't worry about forming full sentences and correct spelling.
- ⊙ Watch out for AOLs - nouns, distinct images or pieces of information that just seem to be fitting together too well. Record, but as AOL, and take a break to clear your mind before continuing.
- ⊙ Sketch and probe your sketches, with the intention of gaining information about the target.
- ⊙ *The information is already out there; all you have to do is write it down! Remember, you are not limited by space, time, target size, shielding or distance!*

Now, do the exercise by following the instructions below. If you'd prefer to read through this section first, read up to the 'Well Done!' heading, then come back and do the exercise.

Preparation

It may be useful to think of the pre-remote viewing preparation as not just simply recording the administrative information useful for tracking when the session took place, but also as a part of the cool-down. With intention, you can give the set-up procedure a sense of importance: imbue the process with the sense you are about to embark on a meaningful exercise. With repetition, the process itself will reinforce this sense back to you.

Get a pen, preferably black, and paper, preferably white and unruled. Sit comfortably, preferably at a table, in a place where you will not be disturbed for 20 minutes (so you may want to turn your phone off). Write your name down in the top right of the paper; under that, write your location (just the town or city will do) and, under that, the date.

Under this, draw a vertical line down the length of the page, about an inch and a half in from the right side, and label the top of this column 'AOL'. Now put your pen down.

Your name

Your location

Date

AOL

The Cool-down

Run through your own process to get yourself into a calm, relaxed state. Listen to some relaxing music, or just sit quietly and focus on your breathing. Let any thoughts that come to mind float by and bring your attention back to your breathing.

Acknowledge and set aside any concerns that are on your mind by asking that they not disturb you from your work. Say to yourself, *'For the duration of this session I set aside...'*, and name anything that is playing on your mind. For example: *'I have slight backache and I can hear traffic outside, I will set these things aside for the duration of this session so I will not be disturbed by them.'*

Set your intention and expectation. Say to yourself: *'My intention is to connect with the target and describe it in detail. I will supply useful information as requested by the tasker. I will have a successful and fun session that I will learn from.'*

Feel yourself drifting towards your 'no expectation' state and become attuned to what you are sensing and feeling.

Lose any preconceptions about what the target could be. Be open to all possibilities. Lose the need to name the target.

When you feel ready, note down the time under where you wrote the date and begin the procedure.

1. Relax

Relax, take some deep breaths and close your eyes. Use whatever technique you prefer in order to clear your mind. Go to your 'no expectation' place using a method that suits you. Become aware of your own internal state. Stay here as long as you like. When you feel ready, move onto the next step...

2. Prompt

When you feel ready, pick up your pen and write the time under the date, and the target number on the left side of the page. As you write, say the target number out loud, *'Target RVPG Y171'*. These acts underscore your intention to bring your awareness to the target and make a connection with it.

	Time
RVPG YI7I	AOL

You are at the location! What do you feel?

The first time through the process, sense any initial impressions.

Subsequently, use this step to individually query each of your senses, and then each of your questions. Prompt yourself with clear and specific commands for information.

3. Listen

Now move from the state of 'no expectation' to a state of expectation - you have asked a question and you now expect an answer. Experiment with the long and short approaches to the 'listen' step.

4. Become Aware

In a relaxed, open state allow an impression of the target to enter your awareness. If nothing happens, remain relaxed and try the prompt again. If still nothing enters your awareness, prompt with your next sense or ask your next question. As soon as some feeling or perception makes itself known, immediately move on to the next step.

5. Record

Write it down, say it out loud.

Record, don't analyse.

Describe, don't name.

Keep anything that could be AOL off to the AOL column on the right-hand side of the page. Remember to take a break; put your pen down, clear your mind and, when you feel ready, pick up your pen and continue.

Repeat the Steps

After capturing your initial impressions, repeat the procedure to run through the prompts listed below to query your senses, get a sense of space and dimension and make a sketch, then move onto more complex information such as the target's purpose.

During the 'relax' step, be conscious of getting into the 'no expectation' state before moving onto your next prompt. Only when you have cleared your mind should you move onto the next prompt.

As you work through the prompts, repeat the TRN as often as you feel necessary to reinforce your intent and re-affirm your connection with the target, e.g., *'RVPG Y171, what can I hear?'.*

Command yourself, *you are at the location.*

Anytime you feel the urge to make a sketch, do so.

Intersperse the prompts listed below with time lingering with your awareness at the target and sensing any new information, *'I am at target RVPG Y171, what do I sense?'.*

Suggested prompts:

- ⊙ What do I see? (Colours and qualities of colours)
- ⊙ What can I hear? (Repeat for taste, smell)
- ⊙ What does the target feel like? (Texture and temperature)
- ⊙ What is my sense of space and dimension at the target?
- ⊙ What shapes are there? (Make a sketch and explore the space)

Take the analytical, thinking part of the act of drawing away, and allow the pen to do what it wants, even if it is only a few lines, to capture a shape

Trace over your sketches with the intention of gaining more information

- What is the most representative view of the target? (Make another sketch)
- How do I feel about the target?
- Get a sense of the age of the target (is it old or new?)
- Does the target have any unusual or distinctive features?
- What significance, purpose or use does the target have?

Then, as you know the target is a location:

- Are there people present?
- If there are people present, what are they doing?

Try and ascertain if the target is a structure. If so...

- What materials do I feel?
- Is it natural or man-made?
- Get a sense of the size of the structure (compared to a person, imagine yourself standing next to the target).
- Does it have an inside?

Bring your awareness to the area around the target:

- I am standing at the location, what do I feel under my feet?
- What is the temperature at the location?
- What are the weather conditions?
- What features (textures, colours) does the location around the target have?
- What other elements (natural or man-made) are located around the target?
- In which country or region is the location?

Finally:

- ⊙ Is there anything else about the target that would be useful for the tasker to know?
- ⊙ What else needs to be asked?

The End

When you feel you have obtained as much information as you can from the session, write 'End' and note the time to formally close the session.

You have now finished remote viewing. Consciously detach yourself from the target by doing something else; maybe reward yourself with a cup of tea, you've earned it.

Well Done!

Congratulations - you have just taken a short right-brain vacation.

You are probably keen to see the feedback, but before you do, take a few moments to review and summarize what you have found.

Summary

Remote viewing session transcripts contain a scribbled list of descriptive words and some doodles, which can be confusing for anyone else trying to make sense of them. Full sentences that structure the information logically are a lot easier to read, and will greatly assist the tasker, an analyst or a judge in their role of reviewing your work.

Now that you have finished the remote viewing part of the exercise, you can turn the analytical part of your brain back on to help provide some analysis of what you have discovered, and help with spelling and sentence construction in writing a summary.

Review your session and formulate a narrative about the target. Below where you wrote 'End' and the time on your transcript, write a few sentences that describe the key characteristics of the target. Emphasize the information you feel is most important about the target.

For clarity, split the summary into the different elements that came through in your session, for example, if the target was a location, describe the target itself, its use, and its surroundings in separate paragraphs.

Be careful of using information that you classified as AOL in your summary, as it should be based on the information you received psychically, and not from analysis. If, however, using the AOL best conveys what you want to say about the target, state it in terms that make it clear that you recognized it as AOL, for example, 'The target's structure reminded me of the Eiffel Tower'.

Now, review the target feedback to see how you did.

Feedback

Don't look at the feedback until you have completed your session.

Go to www.NaturalRemoteViewing.com and select 'Targets', from the menu.

Look down the list of TRNs, or use the Search function, and click on the link for TRN **RVPG Y171** to display its feedback.

The object of the exercise was to run through the procedure. No prizes at this stage.

Study your session in comparison to the feedback. Be sure to read any feedback text, as well as viewing the pictures. You may want to search online for extra information about the target you perceived during your session that was not provided as part of the feedback. (For example, you could use a map to see if a structure is near water, if that is what you recorded.)

Celebrate anything you described correctly. Make a big deal of it, congratulate yourself. You and your subconscious will like this and will look forward to receiving praise in the future.

If the target is not what you thought it was, do not be disappointed; what you thought the target was would have been based on left-brain analysis, which is not the point of remote viewing. Specifically naming the target is not the goal here - it would be very good if you did, but the role of the remote viewer is to describe, not name. This was an exercise in which to learn the remote viewing procedure. What with the procedure itself and the preceding information, there was a lot to think about - and having a lot to think about is not conducive to remote viewing. The psychic signal is subtle and fleeting, and can easily get lost, and incorrectly interpreted.

It is easy to say you have failed if you did not 'get' the target, but look at the descriptive words you used and compare them to the feedback; you will see things that are correct. Recognizing there is correct information, and there will be some, is an important step in learning.

This process was an opportunity to try-out the procedure. How did you feel during it? Hopefully, you were relaxed and not paying attention to how you were feeling. Perhaps you felt anxious, unsure of what to do and frustrated as nothing was happening. Throughout a remote viewing session, you either need to feel at rest in a relaxed, open state of 'no expectation' or engaged in the process. Try and avoid anything that disturbed you enough to move you out of these states in future practice.

You may have felt yourself wanting to rush in order to finish and see the feedback. Try to set this feeling aside and focus on the process. Once you see the feedback, you may feel that, had you spent more time on it, you could have retrieved more information.

You may have felt you were not 'getting' anything. This may cause a sense of pressure and a feeling that you cannot do this. This is not the optimal state for remote viewing. The solution for this is to treat the process as an exercise in relaxation. In your next session, make the relaxation aspect the focus of what you are doing, concentrate on your breathing, and slowly work through the procedure, but as an exercise in meditation, not an exercise in getting something right. It does not matter whether you are right or wrong; you are relaxing and learning.

Bear in mind that remote viewing is very far from 100% accurate, 100% of the time. Even the best, most experienced remote viewers have off days and miss the target. It is fine to be incorrect. Remote viewers should not fear failure; there will be 'missed' sessions and disappointment. Ego needs to be set aside, and practice maintained, approached with an attitude of compassion for yourself. Apply what you have learnt to your next session.

'A Procedure for Remote Viewing' Section Summary

- ⊙ Preparation: give yourself time and space to perform an unrushed session.
- ⊙ Preformat your page with your name, location, the data and time, and the AOL column.
- ⊙ Cool-down to attain a state of 'no expectation' and become a 'blank slate'.
- ⊙ Set aside any concerns that are playing on your mind and set your intention and expectations.
- ⊙ Set your intention to make a connection with the target and write down the TRN.
- ⊙ Relax > Prompt > Listen > Become aware > Record.
- ⊙ Relax:
  - o Put your pen down and move your awareness away from the target, clear your mind. Be the state of 'no expectation'
- ⊙ Prompt:
  - o *You are in the presence of the target*
  - o Ask your question
  - o Use the TRN to 'connect' to the target

- o Query senses, spatial and dimensional aspects, your own feelings about the target, and anything that you feel needs to be asked
- ⊙ Listen:
  - o Expect an answer
  - o Experiment with the long and short approaches to the 'listen' step
- ⊙ Become aware:
  - o What are you sensing?
  - o Watch for and record AOL to set aside potential interruptions from analytical thinking
- ⊙ Record:
  - o Describe, don't name
  - o Record, don't analyse
- ⊙ Formally end by writing 'End' and the time and disconnected from the target.
- ⊙ As good practice, review your completed session and formulate a summary, structuring the information into a logical narrative. Anyone reading your transcript, including you in the future, will appreciate this.
- ⊙ Make the remote viewing procedure your own, use the Relax > Prompt > Listen > Become aware > Record steps when you need to.
- ⊙ Review the feedback, and supplement with your own research.
- ⊙ Find correlations with the feedback; even when it seems you missed the target, there will be some correct information.
- ⊙ Celebrate any correct descriptions.
- ⊙ Even the best remote viewers have off days.

Practise, Practise, Practise

There is a well-known 'first-time effect' in remote viewing practice.[44] The observed pattern is that a beginner's initial sessions can sometimes show uncanny accuracy, instilling a sense that remote viewing is an easily repeatable process, only to be followed by disappointment, as later sessions fail to live up to these expectations. This may cause the viewer to think their initial success was a coincidence, that they really cannot do it, that remote viewing doesn't work. However, with continued practise quality is seen to return and become more consistent.

As with a lot of things, such as learning how to ride a bicycle, playing the piano, or practising a martial art (remote viewing is often referred to as a martial art for the mind), the way to improve is to stay at it.

Practise includes getting into the remote viewing mindset through your cool-down process and taking time to study your feedback and look for correlations – even when your initial view of the feedback makes you think you are way off, you will find information that matches the target.

As you practise, change your approach to make it work for you. Maybe alter your cool-down procedure, spend more time at the 'relax' step, or modify your prompting. Make the procedure your own; the steps I have described are not a rigid framework, but a guide to help you on the way. It is there as a tool to get you started, and help when it seems nothing is happening. Think of it as a set of training wheels; with practice, the process will become automatic and the training wheels can come off, and you'll be free to go and explore at your own pace, using your own process.

You may find impressions coming to you without your prompting and having time for the 'listen' and 'become aware' steps. As always, do not analyse, just accept them, with thanks, and write them down.

Prior to beginning a session you may feel a build-up of performance anxiety. You need to work through this; do not fear failure. Do not force yourself if you are not in the right frame of mind, or do not have adequate time; a rushed and subsequently poor session will not provide a positive learning experience. But do try and get into the habit of doing a session when you have time. A 10-minute session with nothing more than a few minutes of a cool-down can still produce good results and be good practice.

Practice Targets

Before reading the More Techniques section, I suggest you practise the procedure to get familiar enough that you're not thinking what to do next.

Here are some more practise targets:

Location	RVPG 9781
	RVPG A8Q1
Object	RVPG TP31
	RVPG 8TT9
Event	RVPG H009
Person	RVPG A019
No front-loading	RVPG FD61
	RVPG 88A1
	RVPG P121

Ongoing Practise

I post a new target TRN on the Targets page of www.NaturalRemoteViewing.com once a month or so, and post the feedback a few weeks later. I announce these events on the Facebook group for the book: www.facebook.com/groups/NRVBook/

There are several other sources of targets online similar to the Natural Remote Viewing practise target list (see the Websites section; in particular, the 'ONE20+' site has a section that lists sites with practice targets, as well as sites with example sessions). The remote viewing example below contains a walk-through of using the RVTargets.com site.

Alternatively, you can ask a friend to act as a tasker and create a pool of targets for you. When you are not around, ask them to find a set of interesting photographs (a varied selection of people, things, natural settings, animals, man-made structures etc. using the guidance in 'What Makes a Good Target?') and put each one in an envelope. For each target, they will need to generate a unique TRN of their own design and write it on the outside of each envelope.

With no specific question, the implied task would be to describe the image in the photograph from the viewpoint of the photographer at the time the picture was taken. However, a more particular tasking could be requested by the tasker with the addition of a specific question, written down and placed inside the envelope, alongside the photograph. For your practice of remote viewing, these extra enquiries should be unambiguous and not too complex, they should be questions for which the answers are known, for example, '*London Eye - describe the purpose of this structure*'.

Your tasker could also find interesting objects, hide them from you and ask you to describe them.

What Makes a Good Target?

Good targets are interesting targets. Things that we find interesting in real life are likely to be interesting to us psychically.

The same goes for things that we do not like, or are afraid of. I would not be happy if I was tasked with a target of a box of spiders. (There are no disturbing images in the practice targets on the Natural Remote Viewing website.)

As we are using our senses and will use descriptive words and sketches to capture our impressions, scenes that have interesting or unusual shapes will make good targets.

Our interest is sustained by movement or change. Even though photographs are static images, if the actual scene had movement or some energetic element, it would tend to be a more interesting target than one without.

A photograph of a mundane street scene or a field of wheat would be difficult to remote view, as these images would hold no interest for the viewer. With no attention-grabbing centre of focus, these types of scenes would make poor practice targets.

Actual physical objects will make better targets for training purposes as they will give more tangible feedback for the senses in terms of texture, weight, colour and shape compared to photographs.

In 1988, as part of her paper, *Characteristics of Successful Free-response Targets: Theoretical Considerations,* Caroline Watt of the Koestler Parapsychology Unit at the University of Edinburgh, reviewed the literature available at the time that made recommendations of targets for ESP practise. Assessing these from the viewpoints of psychology and parapsychology, she recommended that targets for free-response research should be 'psychologically salient and physically salient', that is, they should contain elements that held human interest, such as being emotionally charged, have interesting shapes, contrasting forms, novelty or movement.[45]

Are We Viewing the Photograph or the Target Itself?

Is the remote viewer viewing the static feedback photograph or the place/event itself? There is some debate about this. However, do not limit yourself; it will be beneficial to think that you have access to both, allowing you to describe the picture in enough detail for you to claim an obvious hit, and to pick up information from the location itself, not accessible from the photograph, such as smells and sounds.

Experiment with your intention by wording your prompts to specifically view the photograph or the place/event shown in the photograph and see what results you get.

The tasker should also be specific in their intent and tasking. If the actual location, object, scene or person is the target, and the photograph is a representation for feedback purposes (the specific photographic image is not the actual target), this should be stated in the task, e.g., 'Describe the actual object shown in the feedback picture'.

Whereas the task 'Describe the image shown in the photograph you will see' would be more useful in ARV exercises, where the goal is to clearly identify one photograph from another.

Outbounder

An additional type of remote viewing practice you can do with another person is the 'outbounder' or 'beacon' experiment.

At a pre-arranged date and time, your friend visits an interesting location of their choice. Following the remote viewing convention, you are 'blind' to the target, so the location is not known to you. Your friend, the 'outbounder', should stay at their chosen location for at least 15 minutes. They should walk around and take it in, fully experiencing it with their senses. They should also make some notes on what they saw, sensed and felt, and take a few pictures.

At the same time, you perform your session. Your job is to describe the location, with your intent focused on the current location of your friend. They are acting as a 'beacon' for you to focus your attention on.

After the allotted time, and after you have completed your session, you meet. Ideally, you should then both visit the outbounder's chosen location. If this is not possible, your friend's notes, pictures and recollections will act as your feedback. Compare the impressions of your first 'visit' - your session - to the actual location and the experience of your friend. This is excellent direct feedback.

Here is an example from the RVPGNYC Group where a member, acting as an outbounder, visited Madison Square Garden, before joining the meeting that was in progress.

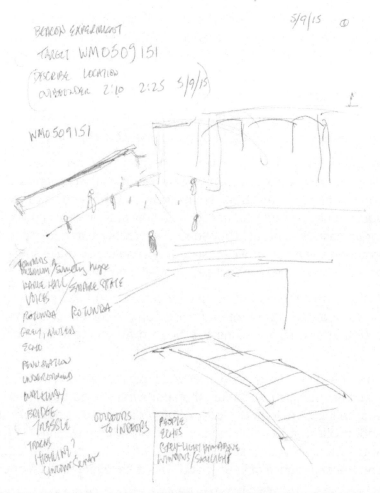

The viewer tracked the transition of the outbounder from 'outdoors to indoors', 'towards a museum / something huge' to a 'large hall' or 'rotunda'. 'Underground' and 'Penn Station' are also mentioned.

The outbounder was one of the main experiments in the early days of the research at SRI and is described in *Mind-Reach: Scientists Look at Psychic Abilities*. When the SRI experimenters travelled away from the office, they took the opportunity to continue the outbounder tests, sometimes involving distances of thousands of miles between the viewer and the outbounder. These experiments showed no lessening of accuracy due to distance.

Join a Group

I found there seemed to be a difference between when I tried online practice targets on my own and when more people were involved (either the tasker or more viewers at the same target). As part of a group, I felt a commitment to be involved and so was more engaged. This encouraged me in my practise and subsequently I seemed to do better. This is why I started the Remote Viewer's Practise Group – NYC (RVPGNYC), to meet with others interested in discussing and practising.

RVPGNYC is run through www.meetup.com. Meetup.com provides online tools for running any type of group, allowing group organizers to easily arrange meetings and keep members informed of group activities. Becoming a member of Meetup.com is free (meeting organizers are charged). As a member, you will find local groups for everything from photography to ballroom dancing. You will probably find groups for meditation practice, as well as for your own hobbies and interests. There are several related to remote viewing. If there is no local group in your area, think about starting one! (That is what I did. Contact me; I would be happy to pass on my experience.)

There are also online communities where you can take part in group practice sessions, and see how others work, ask questions and take part in discussions. I would recommend the TKR Forum (see the 'Websites' section), where you will find other viewers' sessions, as well as experienced and friendly viewers who will be happy to discuss any aspect of remote viewing. Alternately, or additionally, ask a friend to assist. They could act as a tasker, to find and assign targets to you, or as a monitor (See the 'Roles' section), to help you get set up and walk you through the session.

Online Practice Target Example

Here is a walkthrough of how to use the www.RVTargets.com site to assign yourself a new practice TRN and, later, to retrieve the target's feedback photograph.

This site contains a pool of targets. You can request up to three TRNs at any one time.

Later, after you have completed your session, you can view the target's feedback picture using its reference number.

I have included a sample session on a target from the site.

Requesting a Target Reference Number

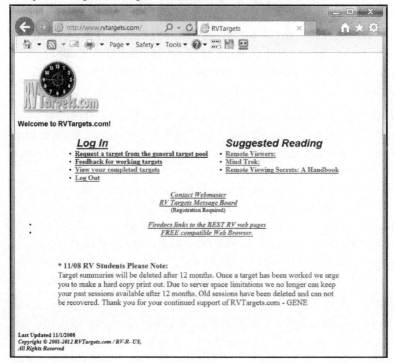

You need to register and log in with your email address.

Login To RV Targets

Enter your E-Mail Address and password and we'll set a cookie so we know you're logged in.

Email Address:

Password:

[Login To RV Targets]

[Register A New Account]

[Change Your Password]

[Change Your Email Address]

[Forgot Your Password?]

Once logged in, you'll have the option to request a target reference number.

Total Private Targets Worked: **0**

Total Public Targets Worked: **0**

Total Working Targets: **0**

- **Request a target from the general target pool**
- Feedback for working targets
- View your completed targets
  Print out for your records
- Log Out
- RV Targets Home Page

Click *Request a target from the general target pool* and you will receive a new target reference number.

Your new Target ID is **RVGxxxxxxxxxx**

Make a note of this reference number, and perform your session.

Remote Viewing Session and Summary

Here is an example session and summary:

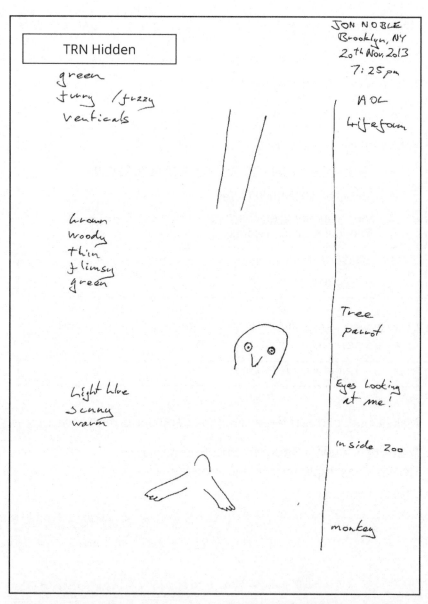

TRN Hidden

green
funny / fuzzy
verticals

brown
woody
thin
flimsy
green

Light blue
sunny
warm

Jon Noble
Brooklyn, NY
20th Nov, 2013
7:25 pm

AOL
Lifeform

Tree
parrot

Eyes looking
at me!

inside zoo

monkey

Green / Furry / Fuzzy / Verticals / AOL Lifeform / Brown / Woody / Thin / Flimsy / Green / AOL Tree / AOL Parrot / Light Blue / AOL Eyes looking at me / Sunny / Warm / AOL Inside Zoo / AOL Monkey

Almost immediately I had the impression of a life-form. I put this into the AOL column and took a break. I returned to the target with the intent to focus on adjectives. I only managed a few more descriptive words before I was drawn back to naming, categorised as AOL, and the sense of being stared at.

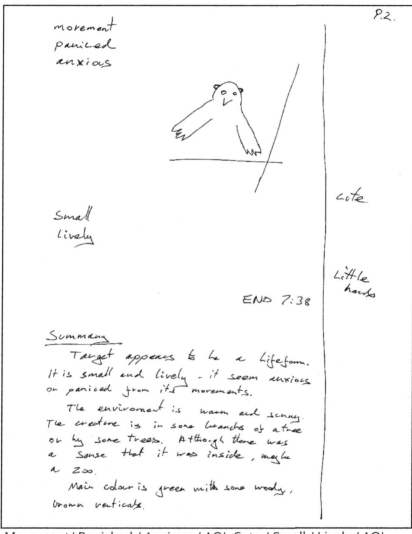

Movement/ Panicked / Anxious / AOL Cute / Small / Lively / AOL Little hands

Summary: Target appears to be a life form. It is small and lively – it seems anxious or panicked from its movements.

The environment is warm and sunny. The creature is in some branches of a tree or by some trees. Although there was a sense that it was inside, maybe a zoo.

Main colour is green with some woody, brown verticals.

Requesting Target Feedback

After the session you'll need to log back into the RVTargets site to see the feedback.

Your current working targets are below.
Click on Target # for feedback.

Target # <u>RVGxxxxxxxxxx</u>

<u>Return</u>

Click the *Feedback for working targets* link and select the target by its reference number.

Are you ready for feedback on Target #: **RVGxxxxxxxxxx**
Requested on: 2013-11-19 21:46:27

<u>**YES**</u> - with Options

<u>**YES**</u> - Feedback Picture Only

<u>**NO**</u>

There is some incorrect, incomplete, and missed data (this is common, for me anyway!). I should have spent more time probing the sketches. However, there is enough here to say that there was contact with the target.

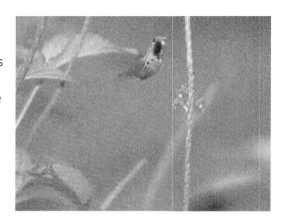

'Practise, Practise, Practise' Section Summary

⊙ Practise the procedure so you become familiar with it - make it your own - before moving on to the next section.

⊙ Practise, practise, practise! Get in the habit of setting 15 minutes aside in your day to practise.

⊙ Find others online, join a group, start a group!

⊙ Practice targets should contain elements that hold human interest, such as having interesting shapes, contrasting forms, novelty or movement.

⊙ A target pool is a set of predefined targets from which the remote viewer can choose.

⊙ The 'Outbounder' is a practice where the viewer focuses their intention on an individual who is acting as a beacon for remote viewing a location.

More Techniques

Now you have your own procedure for remote viewing, here are some other techniques to help you gain more information about the target.

As you practise, take the approach that part of you already knows the answers; you just need to write them down.

Engage Yourself

Train the remote viewing system (that is you, the physical being, and whatever or whoever else is in there with you taking part in the remote viewing process) to expect answers to your questions by placing your pen on the paper, ready to write. Make this a habit after the 'prompt' step, and you will be telling your subconscious that you are ready to receive and eager to record.

Take a Break

The opposite of the above is to take a break during the session.

Detaching yourself from the target and making time to clear your thoughts should help increase your ability to discern between psychic information, random thoughts, and AOL.

Ensure each perception you have is from the target, not from your imagination. As you progress through your session, *forget* about what you have written up to this point, so that you do not build on it.

To do this, make use of the 'relax' step in the procedure. You can extend this by simply putting your pen down, moving your attention away from the target and clearing your mind by focusing on your breathing. Relax in your 'no expectation' place.

Re-engage with the target, now with your mind clear, and intention renewed, by picking up your pen and bringing the TRN to mind, or simply by saying 'target' and stating your next question.

You can also take a more extended break; say the doorbell rings or some other interruption occurs, write down 'Break' and note the time. When you return, write down 'Resume' and the time. You're telling yourself and the remote viewing system to pause and restart the process.

If you have not finished the session and feel the break has been too long, it would be better to 'end' it and start another session at another time. Start the second session as usual. Do not try and remember what you had written before, but treat it as a new session. It is likely you will quickly move on to new information from the target, and you'll find your second session complements your first.

Brush-up on Your Vocabulary

A school of thought known as linguistic determinism posits that the words we have available in the language we use shapes our thoughts, and our thoughts shape our reality. Though this concept is not universally accepted, having the appropriate words readily available will make recognizing the things that the words describe more likely. Russell Targ found that learning the parts of the body helped with his medical remote viewing, he felt that 'in order to discern and describe what I was psychically looking at, I should be able to recognise and name it'.[46]

How many textures can you think of? Rough, smooth... anymore? How about prickly, bumpy, lumpy? The list of descriptors below is not meant to be complete, but shows the types and ranges of words available to the remote viewer.

Read through them; some will be very familiar, others less so. As you read, think of their meaning, and also sense them as if you are experiencing them: smell the smells, feel the textures.

The more easily these descriptors come to mind, the less time you will be searching for the right word.

Sense of Smell
What can I smell?
Fresh - Aromatic - Flagrant - Flowery - Sweet - Perfumed
Natural - Organic - Earthy - Wet grass
Oily - Chemical - Gunpowder - Petrol/gas fumes - Burnt - Smoky
Citrus - Lemony - Apple - Peppery - Meaty - Organic - Tobacco - Coffee

Acrid - Fishy - Pungent - Stale - Ripe - Damp - Musky - Rotten -
Decay - Putrid - Rancid

Sense of Taste
What can I taste?
Greasy - Oily
Metallic - Woody - Plastic - Chemical
Bitter - Salty - Spicy - Peppery - Lemony - Meaty - Sweet - Sour -
Sugary - Syrupy - Tangy - Tart - Watery - Zesty
Organic - Rotten - Rancid - Stale - Musky - Musty

Sense of Hearing
What can I hear?
Noisy - Quiet
Banging - Clanking - Cracking - Grinding - Humming - Rattling -
Ringing - Tapping - Whirring - Pinging
Laughing - Shouting - Singing - Talking - Whispering - Moaning -
Groaning - Crying
Barking - Chirping - Cooing - Growling - Purring - Squeaking
Dripping - Sloshing - Gushing - Hissing - Roaring - Splashing -
Gurgling - Whooshing
Echoing - Buzzing - Clicking
Rustling - Rasping
Jingling - Ringing - Chiming
Rattling - Rubbing - Rumbling - Scraping - Screeching - Slashing -
Smashing - Cracking - Snapping
Thudding - Thundering

Qualifiers: Loud - Soft - Distant - Blaring - Low-pitched - High-
pitched - Muted - Muffled - Shrill - Faint - Deafening - Melodic -
Random - Mechanical - Natural - Rhythmic

Sense of Touch
What textures can I feel?
Smooth - Glassy - Glossy
Course - Dusty - Flaky - Flimsy - Crumbling - Powdery - Gritty -
Bumpy - Lumpy
Flowing - Fluffy - Frilly - Frizzy - Furry - Hairy
Granular - Dimpled - Grooved - Pitted - Reticulated - Uniform
Delicate - Brittle - Fine

Sharp - Jagged - Prickly
Oily - Greasy
Hard - Solid - Rigid - Sturdy - Fixed - Hefty
Rough - Sandy - Scratched
Thorny - Rusty - Textured - Uneven - Weathered - Worn
Silky - Slick - Slimy - Slippery - Damp - Wet - Muddy - Moist - Watery - Dry
Soft - Spongy - Rubbery - Mushy
Plush - Velvety
Feels like: Wood - Glass - Plastic - Stone - Metallic - Marble

Weight: Airy - Light - Heavy

Temperature: Chilly - Cool - Cold - Freezing - Icy - Frigid - Frosty - Warm - Hot - Arid - Burning - Muggy - Sultry – Stifling

Weather: Gloomy - Overcast - Damp - Humid - Wet - Dry - Fresh - Bright - Sunny

Sense of Sight
What colours do I see?
Amber - Beige - Black - Blond - Blue - Brick - Bronze - Brown - Burgundy - Cardinal - Cerise - Copper - Coral - Crimson – Cyan - Fuchsia - Gold - Grey - Green - Magenta - Mauve - Orange - Pink - Purple - Red - Rose - Russet - Rust - Scarlet - Silver - Terracotta - Turquoise - Vermillion - Violet - White - Wine - Yellow

Qualifiers: Patterned - Reticulated - Dull - Ruddy - Light - Vibrant - Bright - Dark - Faded - Pale - Flashing - Cloudy - Dirty - Shiny - Muted - Murky - Milky - Tinted - Mottled - Piebald - Glistening - Glowing - Shimmering - Glittering - Twinkling - Misty - Vailed - Obscured - Shadowy - Shady - Spotted - Reflective - Clear - Opaque

Sense of Dimension and Spatial Awareness
Regarding shape, are there any horizontal, vertical or diagonal spatial elements?
Shape: Straight - Linear - Angled - Angular - Square - Peaked - Pointed - Forked - Flat - Oblong - Oval - Spherical - Circling - Circular - Crooked - Curved - Rounded - Boxy - Rectangular - Triangular -

Pointed - Horizontal - Vertical - Diagonal - Perpendicular - Steep - Slanted - Tapered - Wavy - Tubular - Reticulated - Rolling

Relative position: Above - Below - Close - Distant - Near - Far - Adjacent - Inside - Outside - Under - Over - Up - Down - High - Low - In-line - Staggered

Size and dimension: Big - Small - Broad - Wide - Cavernous - Gargantuan - Gigantic - Huge - Immense - Massive - Vast - Miniature - Fat - Slim - Puny - Petite - Slight - Tiny - Thick - Thin - Tall - Towering - Long - Short - Narrow - Squat - Trim - Wide

Density: Dense - Solid - Hollow
Sense of depth: Shallow - Deep
Sense of space: Spacious - Open - Airy - Cramped - Cluttered - Condensed - Busy - Sparse - Stark – Barren

Brush-up on Your Sketching

If you lack confidence in your ability to sketch, as this was something you were never good at, you may not feel comfortable sketching during your remote viewing sessions. Don't be; sketch away. Sketching is an important part of the remote viewing process as it builds your connection with the target.

However, you may want to invest a little time in reviewing some 'how to draw' tutorials available online and practise a few simple sketches of items in your home as an exercise in getting your arm moving. Hold off from judging your results - do not listen to the part of you that says you cannot draw.

A recommended resource is Betty Edward's *Drawing on the Right Side of the Brain*. The book, which was used in the military remote viewing unit as a teaching aid, takes an innovative approach to drawing by having people break out of left-brain ways of seeing - a good thing for a remote viewer to do.

Sketching Faces

Something many of us are not good at, and do not even attempt for fear of what a poor job we will do, is draw faces. However, it is essential for describing people; you may not be winning prizes in a drawing competition, but you will be making contact with the target.

Help is at hand; there are many books and videos available that can teach you how to draw faces.

Psychic artist Christopher Barbour works with crime victims' families and law enforcement, as well as teaches at the School for Psychic Studies in Massachusetts. His sketches are remarkable for their accuracy. The example shown here, a 100-year old case, illustrates how time has no bearing on clear intuitive hits. As Christopher says, *'If intuition is a timeless perception of truth or truths, then time doesn't sabotage our potential clarity... unfortunately mythologies in our heads can.'*

You can see more examples on Christopher's Facebook page.

He has a simple piece of advice for sketching faces: start with one eye.

A common approach is to sketch the outline of a face, then fill in the facial features. An issue with this method is that you will need to size the features to fit the outline of the face you have drawn. This will take some skill and practise, and you may spend more time making the feature fit than in the relaxed, focused state required for remote viewing.

However, if you start with an eye, you will be able to use its length as guide to define the position of the other facial elements, as they, very generally, fit as follows:

- The eyes are an eye-length apart (the 'A' line), and the side of the head is an eye-length from the edge of the eye. The ear extends out from the side of the head, and up slightly from the centre line of the eyes.

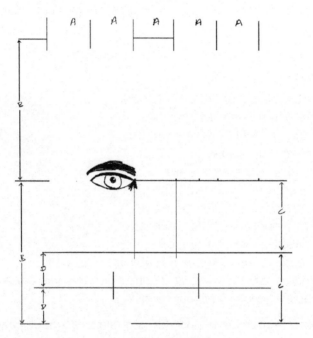

- The head is 5 'A' / eye-lengths wide.
- The eyes are midway between the chin and the top of the head (the 'B' lines are the same length).
- The bottom of the nose is midway between the eyeline and the chin (the 'C' lines are the same length).
- The edge of the nose, at the bottom, aligns with the middle 'A'.
- The mouth is midway between the bottom of the nose and the chin (the 'D' lines are the same length). The corners of the mouth align with the pupils.

Christopher explains his approach and process on a DVD recorded at the 2014 International Remote Viewing Association Conference: 'Sketching Human Faces for Remote Viewers' (available through the International Remote Viewing Association's website).

Probe Sketches

No matter how good or bad you feel your sketches are, and even if you do not know what you have sketched, any sketches you make can be 'probed' for more information. Think of your pen as a stylus or probing tool, and your sketches as two-dimensional representations of the actual target that you can use to navigate around and explore the target to obtain more information.

After the 'relax' step, place and hold your pen on a line you have drawn, and wait and see what comes to you. Pause for a number of seconds; with the expectation of receiving new information from that specific part of the target. If nothing comes, then ask a specific question, for example, 'What does this feel like?' 'What colour is this?' And so on, as you feel necessary. Move the tip of your pen to another part of your sketch and perform the same exercise. Write down everything that comes to you.

With the intent of *feeling* the target, run your pen above the drawn lines. You may feel you want to redraw parts of your original sketch, based on a new sense of the target. Examine each component, and the areas in-between. In any given sketch, there are at least two distinct areas to investigate. Even a single line, taken as a boundary, has the area inside (or one side of the boundary), the area outside (or the other side of the boundary), and maybe a third area in the boundary itself, each of which may warrant its own description.

Label these areas with letters, i.e., 'X', 'Y', 'A', 'B', 'C', as necessary, and describe each of them.

What are these different areas? What are their textures and colours? Are they of different consistencies?

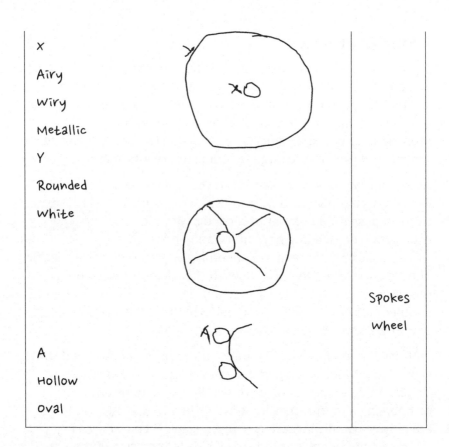

x

Airy

wiry

Metallic

Y

Rounded

White

Spokes

Wheel

A

Hollow

oval

Such probing should trigger further descriptive words and perhaps more sketches, which in turn can be probed - all leading to more information about the target.

Move About

As you are not physically at the target during your session, you are not confined by the laws that govern us in the physical world. Your awareness is free to move around. Take advantage of this by viewing the target from any angle, from up close or further away. If you feel the target has an inside, 'move' your awareness inside and describe what you sense.

To move around the target, state your intended position in relationship to the target, then command your senses to gather a first impression, e.g., *'I am inside the target, what do I perceive?'*.

Make a note in your session transcript that you are looking at the target from a new position. This serves two purposes: you are reinforcing your intent, while also letting anyone reading your transcript know that anything after this point is from this new perspective. Distinguish the text stating the new position from your perceptions by placing it in brackets, such as '(Inside Target)', for example:

	AOL
(Inside target)	
Glassy	
Smooth	
Metallic	
framework	
Rounded	
	cage
curved	
white	

Viewing a target from above and sketching the shapes around the target ('*I am above the target, what do I perceive?*') would be a good way to describe the target's surroundings.

As well as physically moving around the target, you can also move around it in time. Keep your prompts in the present tense, e.g., '*At the time the structure was first used for its intended purpose, what do I perceive?*'.

This ability to move around typically applies to location targets, but viewing objects and events from different angles and at different times could also provide useful information.

Location, Location, Location

Remote viewing is good at describing things, but not so good at locating them. Knowing that the target item is on a 'hard, cold, flat surface' is probably not enough information to be able to find it. Remote viewing's descriptive abilities, however, can be used to put the target in the context of its surroundings.

The guidance in the 'Move About' and 'Probe Sketches' topics above can be used to obtain a description of the area surrounding the target in question. Having the relative location of the nearest road, body of water, or interesting man-made or natural feature would help narrow down the location. This will take practice, but it is worth doing if you wish to use remote viewing in the search for lost items.

Once you feel you have a good description of the target itself using the standard procedure, take a new sheet of paper and, in the centre of the page, make a small sketch to represent the target, with plenty of space around it, which will be used to describe the surroundings. This small target sketch will be the reference point that will provide context for the rest of the information.

Now get your bearings; what characteristics does the target's immediate surroundings have?

Use your pen as a stylus to guide your awareness around the immediate area of the target. What is the texture and colour of the ground around the target? Is it flat or uneven? What questions need to be asked? Write your perceptions down next to the sketch. You will need to return to this location point several times.

The page has now become a map, which you need to fill in. Using your pen as a point of focus and, with the intention of finding new physical elements, select a direction and move your pen away from the small target sketch until you feel something that is different. Make a sketch and describe whatever you have found. If you feel you have found a boundary, such as a road or a river, follow it and draw it in relation to the target.

Return to the target sketch in the centre of the page. Again, using your pen as a guide, go off in another direction. Repeat this process to cover the area around the target in each direction.

You can also give yourself the intent of finding the nearest landmarks, then scan the page for any distinctive feature or structure.

Although you have no indication of north or south, or actual distance (if you feel that you do, then write it down), you will have a diagram of the area surrounding the target in relative distances and directions in relation to the target.

The process described above could be used on a smaller scale, for example, in locating a lost object within a building or room. Focus on the object initially, doing enough of a session to obtain some description of it. Then, on a new sheet, with the missing object represented in the middle of the page, describe the immediate surroundings, including the surface the object is lying on, before finding the shape of the room and any other items in it by using the probing method.

Here is an example; first, the item is described, then the surroundings.

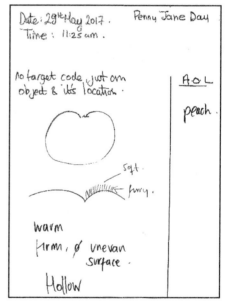

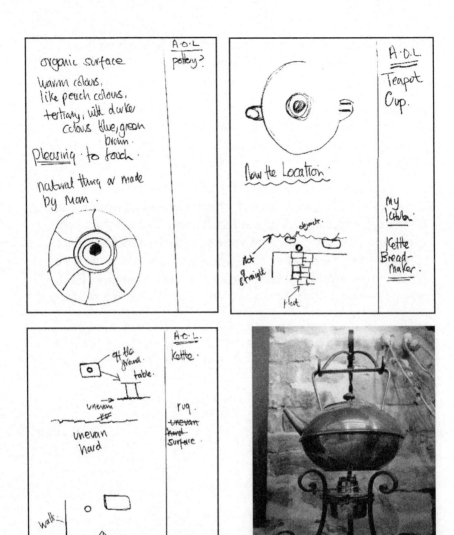

The target was a 'warm-coloured' kettle raised 'off the ground' on a brick surface against a 'uneven, hard' wall.

Ask a Local

So, you've arrived at a new location and are not sure where you are or what's going on. An option would be to ask tourist information or a friendly local, right? You can do the same thing in your remote viewing session. If the target is a location it is likely that there will be other consciousnesses there as well as you; but, unlike you, they are there with their bodies and are visiting the location for its intended purpose - even if it is only the photographer who took the feedback picture you are going to see. Sense if there are people at the target site. If you do sense people, select an individual and find out a bit about them; note their style of clothing, general age and gender, then politely 'ask' them (by setting your intent in your prompt), 'What are you doing here?'. They may ignore you, in which case find someone else who is more forthcoming. Once you have found someone who responds 'see' what they do; they may show you some activity they are involved in, which could give an indication of the purpose of the location. Find out how they are feeling; they may be happy to be there, or they may seem focused and professional in what they are doing. All of this is good information. Record whatever comes to you.

If the target is an object you could question the owner or someone knowledgeable about it. Likewise, with a person target, question them or those around them.

Another Look at Analytic Overlay

Although it is possible that the image or thing you have identified as AOL was a random thought, it is more likely that some aspect of the target reminded you of *something* as it shared some quality or attributes with the target.

That *something* has come more readily to mind, probably as you are more familiar with it. Your left-brain processes have stepped in: analysis, conjecture, memory and imagination have worked out the closest thing it can and provided you with what it thinks is the answer, or something close enough.

Unconsciously, a connection was made between the psychic information from the target and a memory of something that was similar in some regard. It would useful to know what those shared attributes or qualities were.

For example, say that you received the perceptions of 'metallic' and 'thin', and the image of the Eiffel Tower came to mind. You would record this image as AOL, but, before taking a break to allow it to subside, ask yourself why this image came to mind, with the question, 'What is it about the target that reminded me of the Eiffel Tower?'.

If the metallic framework structure of the Eiffel Tower comes to mind in response to this query, then it is likely that this is the characteristic that the AOL shares with the actual target.

Metallic		
Thin		
		Eiffel
		Tower
Framework Structure		

This is good information, which should be written down in the perceptions column on the left-hand side of the page. Now, take a break and clear the AOL from your mind before continuing.

Stay a While

After working on a target for a while you may feel you've retrieved all you can, and you'll start wishing to view the feedback to see how you did. Try and set this urge aside and spend a little more time with the target. You may think that you have received all the information there is and feel that the only thing left to do is end the session. But stay a while, rest in the 'relax' step of the procedure for as long as you want, prompt with the TRN again and linger to allow any new information to present itself. Try this one last prompt: is there anything else I should know that would be useful for the tasker?

'More Techniques' Section Summary

- Teach yourself to expect answers by placing your pen on the paper, ready to record.
- Take a break whenever you want, for as long as you want.
- Taking a break means moving your awareness away from the target. Ensure you do this by putting your pen down and clearing your mind.
- As you go through the process, forget what you have written up to this point; do not build on it.
- Brush up on your descriptive vocabulary.
- Brush up on your sketching, being non-judgemental in your attempts.
- Investigate Betty Edward's *Drawing on the Right Side of the Brain*.
- Learn how to sketch faces. Practise the basic relationships between facial features by sketching a photograph of a face.
- Probe your sketches by placing and holding your pen on a line you have sketched, then wait and see you what comes to you. *Feel it!*
- Move around: view the target from different angles, from up close or further away. If you feel the target has an inside, 'move' your awareness inside. Note the change in perspective, e.g., '(Inside)'.
- Probe the area surrounding the target to describe its setting.
- Find people, start a conversation and ask them about the target - 'What are you doing here?'
- Probe your AOL - 'What is it about the target that reminded me of the AOL?'
- Spend more time with the target. You may think you have finished, but check before you go, by asking, 'Is there anything else that would be useful for the tasker?'.

Remote Viewing Roles

It is possible to practise remote viewing on your own. There are, however, several roles involved in the remote viewing process:

- ⊙ Tasker
- ⊙ Remote viewer
- ⊙ Monitor (optional)
- ⊙ Analyst or judge
- ⊙ Project manager (for projects)

Here is how the process works, and what part these roles play.

Tasker

The tasker's intent is the initial driver for any remote viewing session. The tasker has questions and a desire for information, and so they design a task, which, if performed as requested, will supply the information required.

A TRN is associated with the task and any available feedback for the target is sourced. The target can now be assigned to the remote viewer via the TRN.

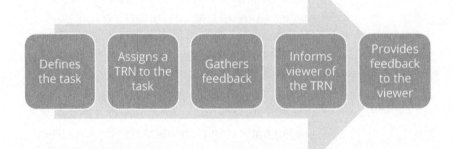

Defines the task | Assigns a TRN to the task | Gathers feedback | Informs viewer of the TRN | Provides feedback to the viewer

Defines the Task

Aside from the remote viewing itself, the tasker's role of setting, and documenting the task is the most important factor in how the remote viewing will proceed. The tasker needs to carefully and purposefully word the task so that it is clearly defined, with no room for misinterpretation. A poorly formed task will likely lead to less than optimal results.

'Describe the object shown in the photograph at the time the photograph was taken' and 'Describe the image shown in the photograph you will see' are both good task definitions for a target, but have different purposes, and could provide different results. The former tasking is looking for a description of the item, whereas the latter, requesting a description of the photograph, would be useful in ARV exercises where the goal is to clearly identify one photograph over another (more on this later in 'The Uses of Remote Viewing' section).

Requests can be open or specific. An example of an open query would be, 'What is the most important thing to know about' a particular concern or area, for example, a specific person's health. A more specific request would be for an answer to a question regarding a definitive topic or aspect of the target. Both types of request would benefit from being framed in the context of any known information, such as a specific time and place, as in 'Describe the location of the person of interest', and specifying the known time of interest / event of interest.

Asking multiple questions in one task is unlikely to provide answers to any of the requests. If several pieces of information are required, it would be better to set up several distinct, but related tasks based on the initial session; for example, if a description of both a person and their location is required, then the initial task should be to describe the person, and a second task should request the description of where the person is. (This could be more efficiently achieved by the use of a front-loaded monitor to guide the viewer to the required information during the session.)

Assigns a Target Reference Number

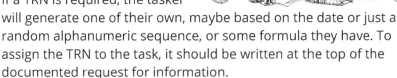

If a TRN is required, the tasker will generate one of their own, maybe based on the date or just a random alphanumeric sequence, or some formula they have. To assign the TRN to the task, it should be written at the top of the documented request for information.

> ## Task 5656/7865
> *'London Eye' - describe from the point of view of the photograph, at the time the photograph was taken.*

If the task is for training purposes, the tasker could also define the appropriate front-loading, in this example, 'the target is a location'.

Gathers Feedback

For training and practice targets, the tasker should also gather the feedback materials that the viewer will be shown after their session. These could be in the form of photographs, text, video, recorded sound, or the actual object, person or place. For operational and research projects, where the answer to the question asked may not yet be available, feedback would be anything that is available that helps to describe the target.

Assigns the Task to the Remote Viewer

Unless a monitor or project manager is involved, the tasker will inform the viewer of the TRN, being careful not to give any indication of the type of target, or any other information that may influence the viewer. The viewer does not see the task at this stage.

Communication to the viewer should be very basic and to the point, along the lines of the following:

The target is 5656/7865.

If front-loading is to be provided, this again should be conveyed to the viewer in a simple message.

The target is 5656/7865. The target is a location.

Provides Feedback to the Viewer

Only after the viewer has completed their session, and no further re-tasking is to be assigned, does the tasker provide the task and feedback to the viewer. If several remote viewing sessions are to be performed, for example, in a large operational project, feedback should not be provided until all sessions have been completed and the project has finished, as any feedback presented during the project would act as front-loading for future sessions.

Remote Viewer

The viewer is informed of the TRN and nothing else (except for front-loading, if relevant). They are 'blind' to the target.

The target is 5656/7865. The target is a location.

The remote viewer needs to do whatever they need to do to get themselves into a state conducive to performing a remote viewing session. This would include setting aside the time, the necessary administrative and mental preparation, formatting the page, establishing intent, and running through a cool-down process of their preference.

When ready, the viewer performs their session. Their role is not to analyse their perceptions of the target and make a determination as to its identity, but to record their experience of it.

For operational targets, and as general good practice, after the remote viewing session has been completed, the viewer should provide a summary of the information they have perceived. This consolidates, formats and logically structures the information felt to be most important by the viewer into full sentences, making the job of the analyst/judge easier.

Once the feedback has been provided by the tasker, the viewer should review it thoroughly. They should supplement the feedback provider by the tasker with their own research to see if their perceptions of the target, not mentioned in the feedback, were indeed correct. Reviewing the feedback aids the learning process, as it informs the viewer as to the accuracy of their session by revealing the identity and characteristics of the target.

The viewer should enjoy their remote viewing successes and reflect on, and learn from, what worked and what didn't during the session.

The tasker plays an important role in the remote viewing process. As the provider of the remote viewing task and associated feedback, the tasker's intent shapes the remote viewer's experience of the session.

The diagram below shows the time-line of events in a standard remote viewing exercise.

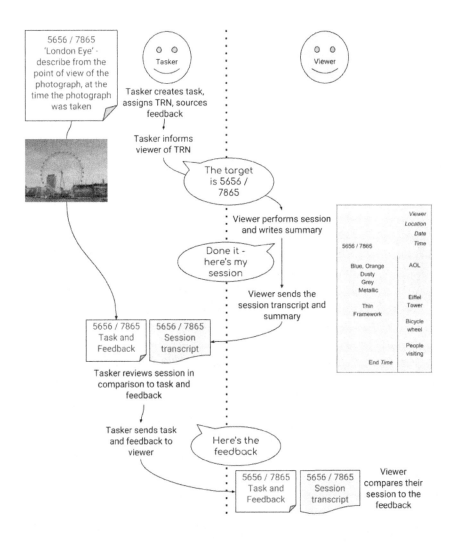

However (it gets weirder), the process is not dependant on the target having been selected before the remote viewing session. As in Dale Graff's future photograph-of-the-day remote viewing where the target event had not yet happened when the remote viewing was performed, it is possible to select the target after the remote viewing has taken place. I do this with my RVPGNYC practice targets: the TRN is announced (on the Natural Remote Viewing website) a month or so before the next RVPGNYC meeting, but the target is not chosen until the morning of the meeting.

Monitor

Optionally, a monitor may assist the viewer in their work by becoming the thinking part of the team, allowing the remote viewer to focus on maintaining a meditative, non-analytical state. The monitor's main role is to ensure that the viewer has everything they need to perform their session, such as writing materials, and anything else that makes the environment conducive to the remote viewing process.

To help things along, the monitor can act as a guide through the process, prompting the viewer, in a quiet way, if there is a sense they are getting lost in the target, such as being side-tracked by AOL. The monitor can also ensure that all senses are queried, and that the target is fully investigated by asking, for example, to return to what seemed like an interesting aspect, which the viewer may have only captured a few details, ('Tell me more about the white circular structure you mentioned') or by suggesting a new perspective ('What does the target look like from above?'). As such, the monitor's role can be particularly beneficial during the viewer's learning phase.

For operational projects and training/practise sessions the monitor doesn't not need to be blind to the target, as long as they do not disclose any information. Having the monitor know the task and the target enough to be able to guide the viewer would be a more efficient way to seek out the required information than re-tasking. For example, if the task was to investigate the activities inside a target building, the monitor could, once the viewer had described the outside of the building, guide the viewer to 'move' inside and describe any movement and activities. Without a monitor, the viewer may be drawn to describe the outside of the location and stop there, missing the task.

In working with a monitor, the viewer should verbalize their perceptions as they arrive as well as write them down. The monitor should not interrupt the viewer and definitely not start analysing and guessing what the target is or ask leading questions. The monitor is there to facilitate; however, the viewer is in control of the session.

Analyst/Judge

The analyst/judge reviews the viewer's completed session transcript.

For practice and training sessions, the judge may assign a score and offer some encouraging and useful commentary on the viewer's transcript to provide guidance for their future sessions.

If the project is using the ARV method (described in 'The Uses of Remote Viewing' section) to make a prediction of the outcome of a future event, it is the job of the analyst/judge to review all the sessions, score them and use their ratings to forecast the outcome, or call a 'pass', if no definitive result can be obtained.

A commonly used ranking classification for scoring sessions is the system developed at SRI.[47] It has since become known as the Targ Confidence Ranking, associated with Russell Targ, as it is described in an interesting paper of which he was the main author. The system defines a range of numeric scores from 0 to 7 based on increasing correspondence between the information recorded by the remote viewer in their session transcript and the actual target, taking into account the amount of incorrect information.

Targ Confidence Ranking System

7	Excellent correspondence, including good analytical detail (naming the target), and with essentially no incorrect information
6	Good correspondence with good analytical information (naming the function of the target) and relatively little incorrect information
5	Good correspondence with unambiguous unique matchable elements, but some incorrect information
4	Good correspondence with several matchable elements intermixed with some incorrect information
3	Mixture of correct and incorrect elements, but enough of the former to indicate that the viewer has made contact with the target
2	Some correct elements, but not sufficient to suggest results beyond chance expectation
1	Little correspondence
0	No correspondence

Table reproduced from *Viewing the Future: A Pilot Study with an Error-Detecting Protocol* (Targ et al., 1995).

As a viewer, you can take on the role of the judge and rate your own sessions. Focus on the recorded perceptions that were correct, and not on what you thought they represented. Your analytical mind will often be wrong in the picture it created of the target, but your descriptions can still be correct. Do not be too hard on yourself, but be sure to be honest - incorrect ranking will not help your learning process.

A more exacting interpretation of the Targ Ranking scale is Alexis Poquiz' Dung Beetle System, used to great effect in the project: *Remote Viewing the Outcome of the 2012 Presidential Election* (Katz & Bulgatz, 2013).

For operational and research projects, where there is more than one viewer involved, the analyst will review the viewer's session along with sessions from other viewers in order to determine themes and commonalities, consolidating the data into a package of information, usually in the form of a report for the client or tasker who initiated the project.

Matching data from several viewers will have more credence than data recorded by one viewer. However, one viewer may have some vital piece of information missed by the others. Analysis of session transcripts is an important and taxing role on large-scale projects.

Re-tasking

After the initial session has been received back from the viewer and reviewed, the analyst/judge may determine that another session could be useful to gather more information about something the viewer described in their first session. In this the case the viewer can be invited to return to the target and obtain more information. This is known as 're-tasking'.

As the viewer has already successfully made contact with the target they can be directly re-tasked, that is the viewer does not need to be blind to the re-task. They are still blind to the target, but now they can be asked to supply more information on something they have already found. Referencing the viewer's own text from their initial session, the viewer is directly informed of the specific element and the area of interest for their second session. A re-task request would be along the lines of:

In your first session, you described a structure and noted 'people visiting'. Please now describe the type of people that visit the location, and what they are doing there.

If the original task had a TRN (say, '5656/7865'), a simple way to generate a new coordinate for the re-tasked session would be to append a few characters to the end of it, e.g., 'r1' (giving '5656/7865r1'as the first re-task request).

Project Manager

On large-scale projects, involving more than one viewer and/or different tasks to capture different aspects of the target, project management-type activities would be required.

These would include tracking which TRNs have been assigned to viewers, which sessions have been received back from viewers, and managing viewer re-tasking. Often, the analyst/judge will take on these types of activities.

It is important that everyone, not just the viewers, but all involved in a project, are working towards the same goal and, as much as possible, have the same intentions and expectations concerning a successful project. To achieve this, the project manager needs to keep project members informed and on board; everyone should know what they are meant to be doing at any given time, participants' concerns should be acknowledged and resolved and, after all the viewing has been completed, viewers should be presented with whatever feedback is available. Lack of communication can create a lack of interest, and the loss of engagement from project members can affect the quality of the remote viewing and so impact the project's outcome.

'Remote Viewing Roles and Targets' Section Summary

- ⊙ The **tasker** records their request for information, clearly as a well-written task, generates the TRN, sources the feedback, assigns the task to the viewer, and presents feedback to the viewer after their session.

- ⊙ The **viewer** receives the TRN as notification of a target. They perform their session, craft a summary, and submit these to the analyst/judge. They then receive and compare the feedback with their session and celebrate any correct information.

- ⊙ The **monitor** assists the remote viewer in preparing for the session and acts as a non-intrusive guide during the session.

- ⊙ The **analyst/judge** reviews the viewer's sessions and may provide comments and assign a score. They consolidate and summarize the findings from multiple session transcripts. For ARV projects, the judge makes the prediction or calls a 'pass'.

- ⊙ The **project manager** organizes the project, assigns TRNs to viewers and tracks sessions and re-taskings.

- ⊙ **Re-task** - The analyst may ask the remote viewer to perform a further session based on their previous session to get more specific information on an area of interest.

The Uses of Remote Viewing

This guide is only an introduction. It has outlined a simple procedure and given you some things to think about as you approach your remote viewing practice.

However, you will not learn how to remote view just by reading about it. The way to become proficient enough to be able to use remote viewing for any purpose is to practise - first to establish the process so that it becomes natural and then to improve in quality and consistency.

As well as gaining a level of proficiency, the remote viewer should also give consideration to the ethical implications of their new skill. The International Remote Viewing Association (IRVA) has ethical guidelines posted on its website, and Joe McMoneagle has a section on ethics in his highly recommended book, *Remote Viewing Secrets*. If you plan on using remote viewing for others, regardless of whether you plan to charge a fee or not, then please read and apply them to your approach to remote viewing.

Find Yourself, Find Your Keys

The biggest implication of any success at remote viewing is that it shows our awareness is not confined to the limits of our physical bodies; we are more than physical beings.

If we can describe locations and objects *blocked from ordinary* physical *perception* by the physical boundaries of *distance, shielding or time*, there is something else going on beyond what we know of our physical reality. For some, this will not be news, but there is a powerful difference between belief and direct experience. This, in itself, will have a profound effect on you and how you view the world.

> *The more and more each is impelled by that which is intuitive, or the relying upon the soul force within, the greater, the farther, the deeper, the broader, the more constructive may be the result.* - Edgar Cayce Reading 792-2

As if that wasn't enough, what are the practical applications of remote viewing?

Using Remote Viewing's Descriptive Abilities

In general, tasks that ask for descriptions and sketches are best suited to remote viewing. As we have seen, and hopefully you have experienced for yourself (or will do if you continue practising), session transcripts produce lists of adjectives and sketches. These can be descriptions of physical items, places and people. Whilst not unknown, remote viewing is not so good at obtaining numbers and text (however, see 'Beliefs' in the 'Mindset' section; whilst working with SRI, remote viewer Pat Price was able to record text held in folders locked in cabinets in a highly secure location). Numbers and text are analytical concepts that are more closely related to left-brain processes, than the right-brain world of remote viewing.

You may be able to find lost items by describing their current location. As per remote viewing protocol, the more 'blind' you are to the target the better, so if someone, say 'Bob', starts asking you to help find a lost item, ask them to stop talking before they give too much information away. Knowing the target is a location and that an object is missing should not hinder the process. You could then task yourself with 'Describe the location of Bob's lost item'.

Viewer Timeline Tasks

I have created a series of tasks that use the viewer's own past/future experience as feedback. They can be found on the Natural Remote Viewing website, in the 'Targets' section.

In order to get the most from these personal targets my recommendation is to give yourself ample time, and to approach the target with an extra sense of purposefulness, in that you will hopefully be gaining some insight into aspects of your own life.

- ⊙ Select one of the targets.
- ⊙ Do your session.
- ⊙ Look at the front-loading guidance and ensure you have covered the items that the task is expecting (for example, your initial session

describes the outside of a structure, and the front-loading states that the 'Target is a structure - describe from the outside and inside').

⊙ If you have not done so in your initial session, redo the task and capture information on all of the elements as specified by the front-loading, and only then look at the task.

I take no responsibility for what you find, or what you do with the information! These targets are provided as practice exercises for your entertainment only. Your actions are your own.

Associative Remote Viewing

ARV is an application of remote viewing that can be used to predict the outcome of future events in situations where there are known possible outcomes, such as in sports competitions (i.e., win, lose or draw) and financial markets (e.g., up a little/up a lot/down a little/down a lot).

To run an ARV exercise, each potential outcome needs to be associated (hence, *associative* remote viewing) with its own target. For example, if two outcomes are to be tested for next week's stock price, will the stock go up or down, two photographs would be required. Photographs are generally used, but objects can be used as well. I will refer to photographs in this explanation.

Before the event, the viewer is tasked with describing the picture they will be shown in the future.

An analyst/judge can then use the remote viewer's session to make a prediction based on a comparison between it and the pictures previously chosen and associated with the potential outcomes. The outcome associated with the picture that the viewer's session most closely resembles is the prediction.

The feedback shown to the viewer is dependent on the actual outcome of the event; it will be the picture associated with the actual outcome, meaning the picture that the viewer will see as feedback is not known until *after the event has happened*.

Let's say that you wished to predict the outcome of a football game that is to be played in the future. If you were tasked with viewing this event directly, you would likely be able to describe people running around a flat, green area, and you may be able to perceive a sense of competition, but it would be difficult to ascertain whom would win, let alone which teams were playing.

This is where ARV can help. In this case, there are two possible outcomes: Team A wins, or it does not (i.e., the other team wins, or there is a draw, or the event does not take place).

You will need a friend to act as the tasker. They should select two photographs, one for each outcome, and associate them with the possible outcomes. These photographs should represent things that are different from each other in as many ways as possible (the fewer characteristics they share, the better); for example, the tasker choses Stonehenge and the Space Shuttle. To associate each photograph with one of the possible outcomes, the tasker should simply write the outcome on the picture.

Stonehenge
Team A wins

Space Shuttle
Team B wins (or there is a draw, or the event does not take place)

The tasker also needs to define the task and assign a random TRN to it, by writing these on a separate piece of paper, for example:

5689 4588
Describe the image shown in the photograph you will see.

Note that the task does not need to mention the game itself or the teams.

All of the activities - defining the task, associating the photographs with the outcomes and creating the TRN - have been performed without you, the viewer, being involved or informed.

The tasker only informs you of the TRN, ('*The target is 5689 4588*'). The remote viewer is blind to the target. You know nothing about the pictures or the task. You don't even need to know that this is for a football match. As far as you are concerned, this is just another remote viewing target.

You don't need to know that this is an exercise in using ARV, but if you did, it wouldn't be a problem. You would know that as the photographs used in the exercise would have been selected as they are sufficiently dissimilar from each other, only a small amount of information is required for the judge to make a prediction. For this reason, ARV sessions can be short, and to the point. The goal of ARV sessions is to allow the judge to distinguish between the photographs, and this does not require the target to be fully explored.

You perform your session. Your summary describes large, grey, cold, stone-like blocks in a flat green landscape. You hand your session transcript over to the analyst/judge (this may be the same person as the tasker, but now they are performing the role of judge). Their job is to compare your work against each of the two photographs. The picture that your session has the highest correlation with would be the pick, and the outcome associated with that picture would be the prediction. In this case, as your session and summary ('large, grey, cold, stone-like blocks in a flat green landscape') has a higher correlation with Stonehenge than the Space Shuttle, the prediction is that Team A will win (as that is the outcome associated with the photograph of Stonehenge).

If a definitive match cannot be found between your session transcript and the outcome photographs, the judge may call a 'pass' - no prediction can be made.

The judge can, and should, inform you of the predication, but you are not shown any feedback at this point because the actual outcome is not yet known. Doing so would interfere with the exercise, as you were tasked with describing 'the image shown in the photograph you will see'.

Only after the game is played are you shown the picture that was associated with the <u>actual</u> outcome, regardless of whether this is what you perceived or the prediction pick. If Team A wins, you will be shown the picture of Stonehenge as your feedback, as this image was associated with the outcome in which Team A wins. If, however, the prediction is wrong, you will be shown the picture of the Space Shuttle. It is important that you only see one picture, the one associated with the actual outcome.

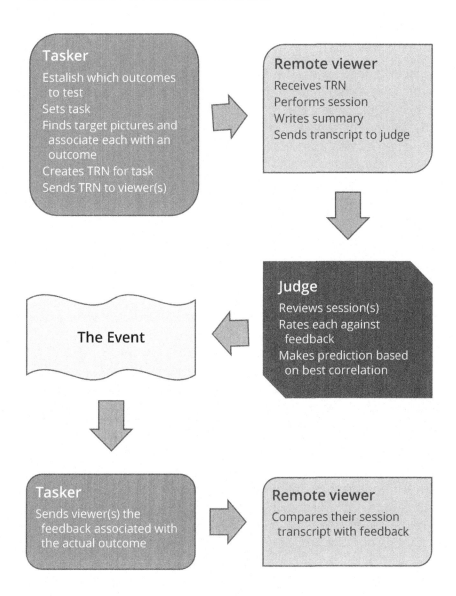

Tasker
Estalish which outcomes to test
Sets task
Finds target pictures and associate each with an outcome
Creates TRN for task
Sends TRN to viewer(s)

Remote viewer
Receives TRN
Performs session
Writes summary
Sends transcript to judge

Judge
Reviews session(s)
Rates each against feedback
Makes prediction based on best correlation

The Event

Tasker
Sends viewer(s) the feedback associated with the actual outcome

Remote viewer
Compares their session transcript with feedback

There is an issue with this type of practice in psi. As there are multiple potential target pictures (one for each associated potential outcome), the viewer can sometimes describe the wrong target, leading to the wrong prediction. This is known as 'displacement'. It may come about as the picture described by the viewer is more appealing or interesting to them, or the other picture, the one they should be describing, holds no interest or is disturbing to them. Displacement is a well-known issue in psi research, being seen in ganzfeld studies as well as ARV. In the use of ARV, approaches have been developed to get around it. Marty Rosenblatt's 1ARV.com is one such approach.

Lincoln Lounsbury has developed a very quick and easy ARV process designed for an individual to use without the need for any other people to be involved. The viewer is able to task and judge the session themselves. The process is called 'QARV', and Lincoln used it to correctly predict winners against the spread in 210 out of 367 of America's National Football League (NFL) games between 2013 and 2016: a 57.2% success rate. His GameDay Psychic website has information on ARV, including an overview of the QARV method.

ARV is often more successful in a group setting with multiple viewers providing sessions, either using the same picture target sets or different target sets for the same task. A number of remote viewing groups, under the umbrella of the Applied Precognition Project (APP), are using predictive remote viewing with a success rate above chance, and are investigating ways to make it more consistently reliable. In April 2016's *eight martinis* magazine, T.W. Fendley reported that the 'Winner Winner Chicken Dinner' APP group had achieved a 90% hit rate for a run of 25 non-pass trials.

Igor Grgić has developed a software program to help manage the ARV process. The program, 'ARV Studio', assists with running ARV trials as an individual or in a group setting. It creates TRNs and emails the group their tasks and their feedback. It also organizes the scoring, provides the prediction and records the project data, simplifying the project management aspects of running an ARV group. The software includes 1,000 target photograph pairs and a target pairing algorithm, which ensures the blind and random selection of dissimilar photographs. It also has a feature that provides predictions based on single sensory perceptions, such as sounds or colours.

It is possible to make money using ARV; indeed, there are several papers that detail the processes used, for example, *Greg Kolodziejzyk's 13-Year Associative Remote Viewing Experiment Results*, and Smith, Laham and Moddel's financially beneficial university project, described in their paper, *Stock Market Prediction Using Associative Remote Viewing by Inexperienced Remote Viewers*.

However, it is also possible to lose money, a large-scale ARV project, designed to predict forex currency fluctuations produced more misses than hits from October 2014 to December 2015, and lost money for its members.[48] Other factors seem to come into play that confuse and disrupt the remote viewing process when financial gain is involved. The title of an article from *The Wall Street Journal* on Delphi Consultants' initial successes with the silver futures market using ARV encapsulates one possible issue: *'Did Psychic Powers Give Firm a Killing in the Silver Market? And Did Greed Ruin It All?'* (Larson, 1984).

Medical Diagnosis

As well as Limitless Mind, there are many books on this topic from authors such as Mona Lisa Schulz, Judith Orloff, and Larry Dossey.

Russell Targ devotes a chapter of *Limitless Mind*, his engrossing overview of remote viewing that covers his own journey through the early days at SRI and beyond, to intuitive medical diagnosis.

As Targ states, using remote viewing for medical diagnosis 'appears to be much easier to do than ordinary remote viewing', possibly because it is 'a more meaningful task than identifying objects and places'.[49] He also found that learning the names of body parts helped 'to discern and describe what I was psychically looking at'.[50]

To get started, the viewer is front-loaded with the fact that the task is an exercise in medical diagnosis, but ideally knows little else about the person, even as to whether they are male or female.

A good approach is to first preformat your page as usual with your name, location, date and time, then draw the basic outline of the human figure in the middle of the page; it does not need to be an accurate drawing, as it is there as a guide to identify the main body areas. Size it so that it takes up less than half of the page, leaving enough space around it to write comments.

Go into your cool-down process and set your intention to help the person by identifying any areas of concern.

When ready, begin the remote viewing procedure, formulate your prompts towards finding not only issues, but also information that will assist in helping the person.

Use your pen as a stylus to direct your awareness to each part of the body (as described earlier in 'Probe Sketches' and 'Location, Location, Location'). Systematically scan each area by feeling / sensing as you go. Use the space around the diagram to record your perceptions.

Before you finish the session, leave with thoughts of healing for the person, and formally end the session in the normal way, making a conscious detachment from the target.

The approach outlined could be used for medical diagnosis of animals.

Before you launch into providing medical diagnosis services, there are ethical and possibly even legal ramifications to offering what could be construed as medical advice, however admirable your intentions may be. Find and consult with others that provide such services.

Helping the Police

This introductory guide is not the place to go into detail, except to say that, if you feel drawn to assisting criminal investigations, you should consult with others that have experience in working on such cases and with the authorities. It is not to be taken lightly. Pam Coronado (IRVA President 2012-2016, star of the popular TV series *Sensing Murder*, runs 'psychic detective' courses, and looking into these, or similar, would be a recommended first step once you have reached a level of accuracy and consistency in your sessions.

Creative Inspiration

As remote viewing can produce descriptive information for targets including people, places and things, and as these descriptions include our subjective thoughts and feelings, could the practice be used as a source of creativity? You may find your own creative ways of using the tools of remote viewing, here is an example.

Participants of the 2014 IRVA Conference were treated to a live rendition by professional cellists of music composed from ideas generated from remote viewing.

This was the first of several creative remote viewing music projects, affectionately known as 'Music from the Fringe', taking place at the College of Idaho. With remote viewing oversight from Marty Rosenblatt, the cellists and composers were taken through an extended remote viewing (ERV) exercise by the group's artistic director, Samuel Smith, and project director, Nancy Smith. The targets were poems by award-winning author Jim Harrison. Following standard protocol, the targets were assigned to the viewers with random TRN coordinates.

On coming out of the hypnagogic ERV state, the cellists were asked to record their impressions and, being skilled musicians, any musical ideas that had come to them. These were presented to two composers, who wove the impressions together to produce the final compositions. Feedback occurred within an hour of their sessions.

A second project was created at the request of Russell Targ, who was very encouraging in the making of the Fringe 1 music. In 2015, Lance Mungia produced *Third Eye Spies*, an action-packed documentary about Russell and the early days of remote viewing. Russell came up with the idea of having music composed via remote viewing as background for the film. Sam and Nancy created the 'Fringe 2 Music Project' to fulfil Russell's request. The selected targets were poems by Robert Frost ('Stopping by Woods on a Snowy Evening' and 'Nothing Gold Can Stay'), each of which was paired with a picture representing the scene described. Five remote viewing cellists, three composers, the artistic director, Samuel Smith, and the remote viewing director, Nancy ran another series of ERV sessions that resulted in producing beautiful and amazingly evocative, lush, and accessible music.

The Fringe 2 music was presented at the 2016 IRVA Conference, along with a showing of the *Third Eye Spies* film. The people involved in these collaborations have claimed that they may have been the most interesting, surprising and rewarding they have worked on to date.

Further Practice, Further Studies

Although capable of providing startling results, remote viewing is not infallible. It is possible to find cases online where remote viewing has not delivered.

Sometimes you just miss, or just get a few things that could be coincidence; I have a large collection of Targ Ranking 1, and 2 sessions, even a few 0's. This happens to even the best, most experienced remote viewers, so you are not alone when this happens to you. If you keep practising, you will astound yourself, and others! There will be sessions that prove the effect beyond doubt; with continued practice, these will likely occur more frequently.

Some believe that practice cannot make you more psychic; this may be true, but learning and practising the tools of remote viewing will help in your discernment of the subtle psychic signal by building your facility to recognize and move on from AOL without being derailed by it, as well as building your resilience in maintaining the meditative, yet focused, state required throughout the session.

To keep your interest, I would suggest working with others; get a friend to help with targets and outbounder experiments. Get involved online, as well as attend meetings and workshops. There are groups looking for remote viewers to take part in projects, in particular, the APP groups. Look on the TKR Forum and the Remote Viewing Facebook pages for projects to get involved in.

Online Tools

As well as practice targets, here are some online tools you may find suited to your style of practice:

Got Psi?

The Institute of Noetic Sciences, the organization started by astronaut Edgar Mitchell, 'dedicated to supporting individual and collective transformation through consciousness research, transformative learning', offers a series of psi activities at www.psiresearch.com. The system tracks your performance (adding to the institute's repository of research data) and automatically adjusts itself to provide a challenging test of your psychic skills.

Russell Targ's ESP Trainer for the iPhone

Originally a large self-contained box of bespoke hardware and software developed in the 1970s used in a year-long project with 145 subjects from NASA, where 'many were able to significantly improve their scores', Russell Targ's ESP Trainer is now an iPhone app. The system presents you with four choices from which to pick. You also have the option to pass. Selecting the right answer, the one chosen by the program, provides you with an encouraging response, so you know you are doing well. The ESP Trainer keeps track of your score.

Recommended Reading

Although reading about remote viewing will probably not make you a better remote viewer, you will learn from others' experiences. Remote viewing has had an interesting history over the last 45 years: from its Cold War-driven government-funded beginnings at SRI and its subsequent research and findings, the military involvement, Stephan Schwartz' work, to the continuation of research at the SAIC and other laboratories and universities, and more recently, the predictive work of the APP.

My suggestions are listed in the 'Recommended Books and Websites' section, while there are plenty of other books, papers and videos available online.

Models of Consciousness

Here is an expansion of the left-brain/right-brain topic, as well as a model of consciousness to help illustrate the concepts behind the remote viewing procedure.

Two Sides of the Brain

By the early 1960s, several people had undergone a procedure to surgically sever their corpus callosum, the band of fibres joining the two sides of the brain, thereby splitting it into two distinct cerebral hemispheres, which no longer have the ability to share information. As extreme as this operation sounds, it was a last resort for sufferers of severe epilepsy and was often successful in reducing seizures.

Roger Sperry and his colleagues, including graduate student Michael Gazzaniga, performed a series of experiments with these 'split brain' patients and found peculiarities indicating that there were specific differences between the two hemispheres: for example, in one such experiment, although these people could name objects presented to the right visual field/left-side of their brain, they could not name objects that were presented to the left visual field/right-side of their brain. It seemed the right hemisphere did not have the words to express itself. The findings indicated that each hemisphere had its own functions and specialized skills.

The work was well received, with Sperry and his colleagues being awarded the Nobel Prize in 1981. The research captured the imagination of the times, and the hemispheric classifications became established in popular culture - the left hemisphere being the logical, analytical part of the brain used in tasks such as language and mathematics, whereas the right hemisphere was the home of the more creative, non-analytical processes, used, for example, in producing and appreciating art and music.

However, further research showed that both physical sides of the brain are involved in each of these tasks and functions, indeed they are required for complete brain functioning. The left hemisphere may be better at language, but it is not a solely one-sided affair. The notion of strict lateralization of function between the hemispheres was largely dismissed and even ridiculed as an urban myth.

Nevertheless, there are distinct physical differences between the two hemispheres, implying that there is something different about them. Iain McGilchrist, in his book from 2009, *The Master and His Emissary*, delved deeper into the topic and offered a broader perspective. It is not that the functions of the brain are split between the left and right hemispheres, but that the two sides are different in how they see the world; they have distinct, yet complementary, points of view and roles.

Simplified, the focused left hemisphere seeks to make sense of the world by identification and classification of each element, whereas the more open right hemisphere looks at the whole - the big picture - and sees beyond the classification to the element in its context.

The right hemisphere works with pattern recognition, shapes and colour, ever scanning the environment for change. The left hemisphere uses analytical processes - classification and labelling with language, in its role to quickly identify and discern friends from threats so that we can navigate our world appropriately.

So strong is the left hemisphere's need to reach a conclusion - to label and explain - that experiments with split brain patients show it will make up far-fetched explanations for actions and reasoning for choices that cannot sensibly be explained, given the information available to it, but which make sense in relation to the information presented to the right hemisphere. This 'left brain interpreter' as Gazzaniga has termed it, is constantly working to make sense of the world, even if that means resolving an incomplete picture by rationalization and conjecture, when not all the information is available.[51]

The issue here for remote viewing is that the left hemisphere's keenness to label and classify, its natural function to reach a conclusion, is based on partial information received via the scant psychic signal. Once labelled and classified, it is difficult for these labels and classifications to be removed. The left hemisphere is focused on its role of classifying the next unknown to ensure that it is not a threat, rather than re-assess decisions already made.

Ψ   *The less the viewer knowns about the target the better, any information can trigger the left-brain interpreter to start building its own model of what it thinks the target is. Remote viewing protocol states the viewer should be blind to the target, and the use of front-loading is minimized.*

Ψ   *In remote viewing the function of naming, so useful in our everyday lives, has a tendency to block further investigation. In fact, yet more incorrect 'evidence' seems to be produced to support the faulty label.*

The remote viewing procedure attempts to get ahead of this inherent naming function of the left-brain interpreter by focusing on target description, and not naming – the viewer's role is to describe, not name.

Another procedural tool to minimize the impact of the naming and classification function of the left brain is to differentiate nouns, and any other perceptions that the viewer feels has come from analytical processing, from other information by categorizing them as 'AOL', and for the viewer to take a break to clear their mind before continuing the remote viewing process.

Ψ   *Remote viewing performance benefits from the analytical processes being held in check, allowing for the subtle psychic signals to register. The optimal environment for this is the world of feeling and sensing that is more the realm of the right hemisphere. Therefore, anything that engages analytic processes, such as analysis, thinking about spelling and grammar, and logically structuring information, needs to be kept to a minimum during the remote viewing session. This is difficult, as in most activities there is a reliance on both analytical and non-analytical functioning. Processing and objectifying impressions from the physical senses, even when perceived psychically, requires the use of some elements of analysis and language. However, with practice the ability to return to, and maintain the meditative state required of remote viewing increases.*

Three Levels of Consciousness

Conscious and Subconscious Processes and How They Build Our Reality

Fortunately, we do not have to be consciously concerned with many of the processes that keep us up and running. These myriad, intricate and important bodily functions, such as the beating of our hearts and digestion, happen below the level of our conscious awareness, in the subconscious. As we have little oversight or awareness of the subconscious, it can seem like another part of us working silently behind the scenes to our benefit, automatically handling many of our core functions, without us having to consciously monitor and regulate them. We may be able to exercise some control over them, but we do not have to; if we do not think about breathing, this other part of us does in order that we continue to live. Included in this are our basic motor functions, such as walking and raising a cup to our mouth to drink; we may consciously initiate the initial command, but we do not need to direct every muscle involved in the process.

Also below the level of conscious awareness we have a vast store of knowledge and experience that may not be accessible at the moment, but can be recalled either by a conscious effort to remember (which for some of us may not work as well as we might like), or some stimulus, such as hearing a particular piece of music or smelling a certain scent. This can sometimes result in a surprisingly vivid recollection of an experience that had not been thought of for many years. It was there all along, stored below the level of conscious awareness.

The initial processing of the signals from our physical sense organs - our eyes, ears, skin, nose and tongue - also happens in the subconscious. There's a number of hoops to jump through before these signals reach our conscious awareness: filters we are not even aware of, which have been put in place as lessons learnt through experience or passed on by those we saw at the time as our teachers; our personal preferences, our likes and dislikes, all interact with the 'raw' data from our sensory organs, interpreting and even editing out content. How tired, alert or distracted by our own thoughts we are affects how much processing power we have available to commit to these processes; if not sufficient, we will simply fail to notice something that may be obvious to those around us.

There is always too much to take in and, as with the ticking clock, repetitiveness is filtered out and eventually disappears from our personal reality.

What appears to our consciousness awareness from the vast amount of information perceived subconsciously, is only the *interesting stuff*. The vigilant right hemisphere is always on the lookout for changes in the environment (whilst the left hemisphere is ready to make judgements). Our attention is directed to things that demand our attention (a ringing phone), as well as anything we are particularly interested in (suddenly you are noticing the car you're thinking of purchasing a lot more than you were before) or we intend to examine.

In this way, attention and intention build our *reality*: an incomplete, yet personalized, world of our own making.

Ψ   *With intention and attention being such powerful drivers in shaping our physical reality, they likely play the same role in shaping our perception of the psychic realm. The remote viewing procedure asks the viewer to focus their intention, and bring their attention to, and query, each sense and each element of the target in turn.*

Ψ *Prior to starting the remote viewing session, the acknowledgement of anything playing on the remote viewer's mind and request that it not to disturb them during the period has the effect of setting it aside.*

Ψ *During the session, interruptions should be minimized; the viewer should find a quiet time and place, and turn off any devices that could make a noise.*

Ψ *If information is not flowing, the viewer should take a break from remote viewing process by moving the focus of their attention away from the target to something else, such as the breath, with a conscious reset to the 'blank slate' state of open awareness. Once this has been achieved, the viewer should refocus on the target. This will hopefully have the effect of presenting the target anew to the viewer's awareness, so they will be more likely to notice the change from one state to another.*

All in all, we are faulty recorders of the real world. An indication of this is the number of cases of innocent people convicted of crimes based on witness testimony, only later to be exonerated by new evidence. Experiments show even the words used in questioning can change people's perception of events, for example, asking how fast cars were going when they 'smashed' into each other resulted in a faster speed being given than when asked how fast the cars were going when they 'hit' each other (see Loftus & Palmer, *Reconstruction of Automobile Destruction: An Example of the Interaction Between Language and Memory.*)

Ψ *The prompts used in the remote viewing process should be open, non-leading questions.*

Superconscious

The following section is indebted to Stephan Schwartz for his presentation of the information regarding Edgar Cayce.

There is a vast history of anecdotes and laboratory-derived data indicating that humans can access and describe information that is *hidden from the physical senses by distance, shielding or time.*

Where is this information coming from? One answer is that it was in the vast store of the subconscious all along, and, like a long-forgotten memory, brought to conscious awareness with intent. This can be surprising for the individual, and may even be used as evidence of psychic abilities, when it is in fact an example of the power of our senses to take in, and power of our memory to store, more than we are consciously aware of.

There are, however, examples of information being accessed that could not have come from the subconscious store, such as remote viewing and ganzfeld studies. Another example is the work of Edgar Cayce, the most well-documented psychic of the 20th century. An uneducated man from a poor farming family, Cayce was able to provide, through his psychic 'readings', accurate medical diagnoses and effective remedies, involving subjects he had no training, or exposure to the level of anatomical knowledge his readings provided. The bulk of his 14,000-plus recorded readings are known as the 'physical' readings, as they concern people's physical disorders and conditions. These provide a large body of information on a wide range of aliments and, because of their general approach of treating the whole body, Cayce is often referred to as the 'father of holistic medicine'.

Other readings covered a wide range of topics as requested by his clients, including financial advice, life purpose, new technological inventions, and treasure hunting. (The original records are kept at the Edgar Cayce Center in Virginia and copies are available online and as CDs.)

Once Cayce became famous, through reports of his astounding abilities in national newspapers (such as the New York Times article from 9th October 1910), he received requests from all over America, so it was usual for the clients  not to be physically present at the time of the reading. For a reading to take place, a prior arrangement was made whereby the client would be in a certain place at a certain time. At this given time, Cayce would loosen his tie, lay down on a couch, place his hands over his chest, close his eyes and enter a trance-like state. When ready, he would be given the name and location of the person the reading was for. Once Cayce confirmed he had *located* the person, he would accept questions. In the room with Cayce was someone to ask questions, normally his wife, and someone to record what was said. The reading would progress with Cayce responding to questions until either all were asked, or he closed the session.

Throughout the readings, there are references to information that is specific to the person at the time the reading was given, such as the person's current state of dress or current surroundings, and, in one case, the fact they were not at the given address at the time (it was later reported they were running late for the appointment). Such information was obviously not available to Cayce, who was often hundreds of miles away from the client at the time, lying on his couch.

The transcripts would be typed up and mailed to the client. Clients, or their caregivers or doctors, often responded, and, from these communications, it is possible to tell how correct the information Cayce provided proved to be. From a review of the readings' transcripts and clients' correspondence, Cayce's sons, Edgar Evans and Hugh Lynn Cayce, estimated the physical readings to be 85% accurate.[52]

Where did this information come from?

Cayce had a dream in which he saw himself as a speck radiating upwards and outwards in an ever-increasing spiral. The journey through the cone was interpreted as the passage Cayce's consciousness needed to travel to access the information required to answer the questions asked by his clients.

A reading was given to further interpret the dream; this stated that the cone represented the connectedness of all consciousnesses, with Cayce referred to as 'the entity', rising up through a 'trumpet of the universe', open at one end, representing access to the universal, the cosmic, the 'heavens itself'.

> ...the entity is - in the affairs of the world - a tiny speck, as it were, a mere grain of sand; yet when raised in the atmosphere or realm of the spiritual forces it becomes all inclusive, as is seen by the size of the funnel - which reaches not downward, nor outward, nor over, but direct to that which is felt by the experience of man as into the heavens itself.
>
> Each speck, as an atom of human experience, is connected one with another as the continuity of the cone seen, and in the manner that the nerves of an animating or living object bears upon that in its specific center, but reaches to the utmost portions of the universality of force or activity in the whole universe, and has its radial effect upon one another. As the entity, then, raises itself through those activities of subjugating or making as null those physical activities of the body, using only - as it were (in the cone) - the trumpet of the universe, in reaching out for that being sought, each entity - or each dot, then - in its respective sphere - acts as the note or the lute in action, that VOICES that which may come forth from such seeking. - Edgar Cayce Reading 294-131

Ψ   *The reading outlines the procedure and the mechanism of Cayce's process, echoing the fundamentals of the remote viewing procedure:*

- *The cool-down, calming the physical - '...making as null those physical activities of the body'*

- *the setting of intention; the act of '...reaching out for that being sought'*
- *and the connectedness of consciousness - the intentions of all play a part - '...each entity...acts as the note that VOICES that which may come forth from such seeking.'*

Cayce's dream and its reading are also discussed in *The Outer Limits of Edgar Cayce's Power*, an investigation by Cayce's sons into information received from their father's readings, which could not be counted as correct. Given the high success rate of most of the material from the 'physical' readings, including some that led to unprecedented recoveries, which baffled medical science at the time, how could some information be wrong?

In Chapter 7, The Nature of Psychic Perception, Cayce's sons propose that some of the readings, in particular, those undertaken in the search for lost treasure, suffered in quality due to the consciousnesses involved; both those living, physically in the room at the time the readings were made, anxious to receive the information, possibly driven by greed, and those discarnate, providing the information, possibly revealing in trickery and deception.

Ψ *Following the dream reading; 'each entity acts as the note that VOICES that which may come forth' – bad notes will affect the voice of the result.*

Lessons here for the remote viewer to check their own intentions; their reasons in undertaking a remote viewing task, recommit to their seriousness of purpose for each session, and to work with taskers of known integrity.

The seriousness of intent of all involved in remote viewing exercises and projects could play a part in the outcome.

Herbert Puryear uses the 'trumpet of the universe' dream and its interpretation as a starting point for a comprehensive set of models of consciousness and spirituality, detailed in his book, *The Edgar Cayce Primer: Discovering the Path to Self-transformation*. Puryear translates the model in various ways, but fundamentally to the three the levels of consciousness, subconscious and a spiritual realm of universal superconscious.

Several terms have come to be applied to the metaphoric concept of a universal superconscious to allow it to be discussed. Cayce also refers to a 'hall of records', and a 'Book of Life', containing all the thoughts and deeds of individuals.

> *Quite suddenly I come upon a hall of records. It is a hall without walls, without ceiling, but I am conscious of seeing an old man who hands me a large book, a record of the individual for whom I seek information. -*
> *Edgar Cayce Reading 294-19*

In the 1880s, theosophists began to refer to the 'Akashic Records', derived from 'Akasha', a Sanskrit word for 'sky' or 'aether'. In the Vedantic school of Hindu philosophy 'Akasha' refers to the essence of all things in the material world.

Students of CRV will be familiar with the term 'the matrix', a concept used to describe the source of data available to the remote viewer.

Carl Jung identified shared themes and ideas amongst humans across history and throughout the world, which led to the formation of his idea of a shared human consciousness.

> *This deeper layer I call the collective unconscious. I have chosen the term "collective" because this part of the unconscious is not individual but universal; in contrast to the personal psyche, it has contents and modes of behaviour that are more or less the same everywhere and in all individuals. It is, in other words, identical in all men and thus constitutes a common psychic substrate of a suprapersonal nature which is present in every one of us. - Collected Works of C. G. Jung, Vol. 9, Part 1. 2nd Ed., 1968, Princeton University Press ISBN 0691018332*

Jung's collective unconscious may or may not go towards explaining psi abilities, but it is an example of a mechanism that facilitates shared information, which has not been learnt or passed on by regular methods of information transfer between us.

A Simple Model of Consciousness

Levels of consciousness are often represented as an iceberg. (Although not the first to do so, Sigmund Freud used the metaphor to illustrate that the larger portion of consciousness was below the surface of awareness. He also used the terms *unconscious* and *preconscious*, which we will not discuss here, nor did he refer to a global or universal consciousness; as such, the following is not Freud's iceberg, just a borrowing of the metaphor.)

Following the 'trumpet of the universe', and Puryear's model, the tip of the iceberg, above the waterline, represents an individual's subjective conscious awareness.

The greater lower portion, residing below the surface, represents the storehouse of the subconscious, its contents unseen and not readily available until some impetus or stimulus makes it so.

The vast sea the iceberg floats in, shown as a larger, open portion, the shared superconscious.

Inverted, it would look like this:

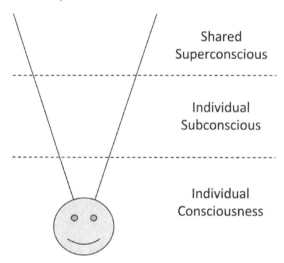

Shared
Superconscious

Individual
Subconscious

Individual
Consciousness

Remote Viewing within a Simple Model of Consciousness

A way of thinking about remote viewing using this model of consciousness is that:

(1) The tasker makes a conscious association between the task, the target and the TRN, and this is placed, by the tasker's intent, into shared superconscious.

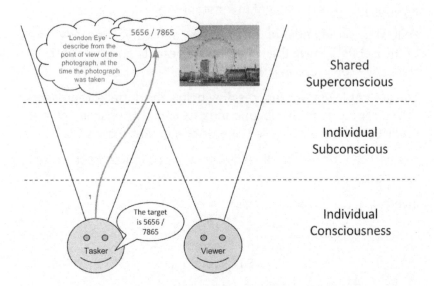

(2) The viewer initiates the remote viewing process by bringing their awareness to the TRN with a sense of purpose - the purpose of retrieving useful information for the tasker. This act of intention retrieves the task from the superconscious and then

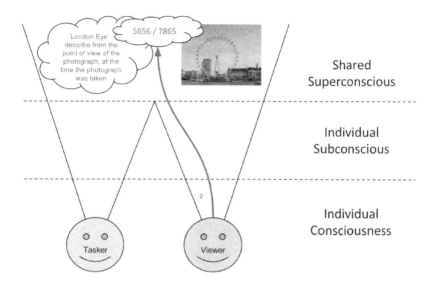

(3) allows for exploration of the subject of the task: the target, by using the remote viewing procedure to specifically investigate its individual elements.

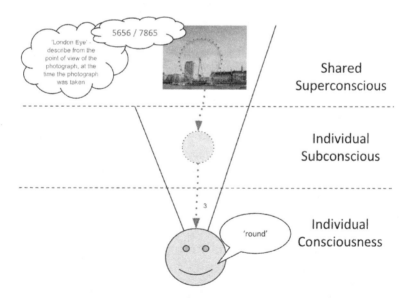

In a state of open awareness - the receptive state with the expectation of receiving an answer, information 'flows' (is made available by some mechanism as yet unknown), from the superconscious, through the viewer's subconscious to their consciousness awareness.

This information is initially likely to be in the form of the language of the right hemisphere: sense impressions, shapes and feelings, available to be 'decoded' via classification and labelling to the language of the left hemisphere, that is, actual words, and, following standard remote viewing procedure, these would be recorded.

Ψ   *It is at the decoding stage, the intersection of the realm of the subconscious and the realm of language and classification, that the viewer needs to be mindful of the influence of the left-brain interpreter, and use the tools provided to minimise its effects.*

Ψ   *Some information may, however, remain in the viewer's subconscious and not reach the point where it can be objectified by consciousness. This information could present itself as an unconscious knowing, which is often how psychic perceptions are sensed. The psychic feels they need to speak out or, in the case of the remote viewer, feels the need to write something down, but does not know why.*

The remote viewer needs to trust and act on this sense (knowing 'the information is already out there; all I have to do is write it down!'), so even when the viewer thinks they have no information (there is no target information in conscious awareness), forcing themselves to write or sketch, with their intent fixed on the target, may allow such 'hidden' information to reveal itself.

If this model has any validity, it seems there is some transfer or extraction of information from superconscious through subconscious to consciousness; maybe it is a shift in awareness to the superconscious, or a channel through the levels. What would facilitate such mechanisms and allow the speck of consciousness to move, as Cayce's did, through the spiral of connected consciousnesses to the level of universal knowledge available to provide help to Cayce's clients?

Factors that Seem to Have a Bearing on Remote Viewing

Here are some thoughts on factors - environmental, procedural, and personal - that may facilitate psychic functioning. You may have you own beliefs in this area; you may need to wear your 'lucky' socks or need a certain phase of the moon. If you have a system that works for you, then don't mess with it, but our beliefs can empower as well as limit us, and testing them will help identify their real power.

Environmental

Removal of External Distractions
Give yourself space and time; a quiet environment where you will not be disturbed. Turn off anything that could make an alarming sound. Ingo Swann asked for a grey room with a grey carpet and furniture at SRI. You do not need to go this far but removing as many external distractions as you can will help.

Quietening of the Physical and the Mental
The ability of the remote viewer to enter and maintain a meditative, relaxed yet focused state is key. Maintaining a regular meditative practice is recommended. A steadfastness of remote viewing practice is required, whilst a certain resolve may be required to overcome frustration.

Prior to a session, the remote viewer needs to obtain the appropriate state; setting aside anything playing on their mind by acknowledging it and asking it stay out of the way, before turning inward to the world of feeling and sensation. Throughout the process the remote viewing procedure provides a number of opportunities for maintaining the required state: the cool-down, the 'relax' step, the break after recording an AOL, and the extended break anytime the viewer wishes to take a break from the process.

Procedural

Adherence to Protocol

Remote viewing tasks need to be planned, unambiguously defined and presented to the viewer without any extraneous or leading information.

Front-loading should be used prudently, dependant on the circumstance, being more appropriate to training and practice sessions. Any front-loading should be concise, speaking in general terms and give no specific information away.

Viewers should follow their procedure, recording the administrative information (their name, location, the date and time) as well as everything that is perceived. The session should be formally closed with 'End' and the viewer should consciously detach him/herself from the target.

These activities should become routine practise, a formula imbued with a sense of purpose.

A well-written and structured summary makes for a better remote viewing product.

Feedback should be available for training and practice targets and provided to the viewer after the session has been completed. For operational projects, any possible feedback should be given to the viewers, but only after the project is complete, when no further sessions will be assigned.

Remote viewing projects need to be planned and run efficiently to be effective.

Use of a Conducive Remote Viewing Method

Viewers should use a method that facilitates open questioning that allows for free-response answers, incorporates sketching, queries all senses, and has a mechanism for minimizing the speculations of the left-brain interpreter, that is, an emphasis on target description and not identification, and a recorded visual separation between information believed to be psychic perceptions and those believed to be analysis and conjecture.

The viewer should have the expectation that the session will be judged as a free-response exercise and not converted into a forced-choice questionnaire (knowing beforehand that certain specific questions will be asked of the remote viewing data will likely affect the viewer's responses).

Mindset of Those Involved

As in any group activity, results come from participants working towards a common goal. Participants should have a shared respect for each other in the process and communicate appropriately. Project managers need to be cognisant of and make efforts to satisfy members' concerns within a project.

Everyone involved should have the expectation of a successful outcome for operational projects and a successful experiment for research projects (even if a successful experiment is proof of an incorrect hypothesis). For research projects, in particular, the double-blind protocol should be used where possible as a guard against potential experimenter effects, such as cueing.

A seriousness of purpose is expected from the tasker as they play such a key role in the formation of the task and sourcing the available feedback, the two core activities that set the tone for the remote viewing project.

Judges also need to take their role seriously, giving each session due attention.

Seriousness of purpose and seriousness of intent do not mean the process cannot be fun. Project managers need to keep viewers and others engaged and motivated.

Personal

Knowledge of Psi Phenomena

Knowing that humans are actually capable of doing the thing you want to achieve for yourself will help in your own efforts.

As an example, running a mile in under 4 minutes had been attempted for several decades, it seemed beyond reach until it was finally achieved by Roger Bannister, in May 1954. Once the 4-minute barrier had been broken, it was surpassed many times in the years that followed, with Bannister's own record beaten just a month after his historic run.

Humans are capable of *the acquisition and description, by mental means, of information blocked from ordinary perception by distance, shielding or time*, and much else besides.

Familiarize yourself with studies of psi abilities. Some excellent overviews of the field are: *The Conscious Universe: The Scientific Truth of Psychic Phenomena* and *Supernormal: Science, Yoga, and the Evidence for Extraordinary Psychic Abilities* by Dean Radin and *The Reality of ESP: A Physicist's Proof of Psychic Abilities* by Russell Targ.

The level to which this knowledge is required may depend on the situation and the individuals involved, being more of a concern in societies where psi is not generally accepted or discussed.

'Permission' to Remote View

An environment where remote viewing is made socially acceptable could be essential. Russell Targ talks of giving his students *permission* to be psychic, allowing new remote viewers to feel safe and secure in what may be the psychological equivalent of walking a high wire, something they have never dreamed they could do, or of actually doing in public.

Having a coach say, 'Yes you can!' (where the prevailing message is 'no you can't, and you're stupid if you believe that') could make all the difference.

Again, the level to which this is required may depend on the situation and the individuals involved, although the opposite - an environment hostile to psi; overtly overly sceptical - would certainly not be conducive to producing good results.

Bolstered Belief

Belief and Expectation play a strong role in psi performance.

The 'sheep-goat effect', termed and first reported by Gertrude Schmeidler in 1947, shows an individual's belief in psi as an indicator to their psi performance. *Sheep*, those believing in psi, tend to perform higher in psi related tasks than *goats,* those who do not believe in psi. Not to say goats do not show psi abilities, they can exhibit evidence of psi by performing below chance. The sheep-goat effect is one of psi's most robust experiments; a recent meta-analysis of forced-choice experiments from 1994 to 2015,[53] concurs with an earlier analysis of experiments from 1947 to 1993, incorporating 73 studies (4,500 participants, 685,000 guesses).[54]

The sheep / goat classification for Schmeidler's initial experiments was specific to the instance of the experiment at hand; subjects were asked, 'Do you accept the possibility of ESP under the conditions of the experiment?'. However, since then the classification is the participant's general level of belief in psi.

Our beliefs, as ingrained as they are, can be bolstered by argument and evidence that supports them, and undermined by argument and evidence that opposes them.

Experiments where the subject is given psi-positive written statements and encouraging verbal cues from experimenters (such as 'we find most people can get good results') show more evidence of psi, than those presented with psi-negative statements and cues (for example, 'we're not seeing any effect with this experiment').[55]

Motivate yourself with your own successes and knowledge that remote viewing is possible.

A Sense of Purpose
Russell Targ's view that medical diagnosis 'appears to be much easier to do than ordinary remote viewing', as it is 'a more meaningful task than identifying objects and places', indicates that the viewer's recognition of the purposefulness of a remote viewing task is a motivating factor. Give some thought to your intentions when performing a remote viewing session; there is purpose in the activity in that you're helping the tasker answer questions, and likely helping those whom the tasker is representing.

You should reiterate this sense of purpose during the procedure by repeating the assigned TRN (or 'target') to yourself and thinking of the tasker's requirement.

As well as enjoying the process as an opportunity to help others, and learn about yourself and how the remote viewing process works for you, you should also set yourself the expectation of finding useful information.

Knowledge of the Topic

We seem to retain our likes, dislikes, interests, talents and expertise when accessing information psychically. Those with some artistic flair, who notice colours and colour combinations, may be better at identifying colours at the target, while those interested in architecture may perceive the definition of structures more readily. This extends to our own lack of knowledge and other deficiencies.

As part of an SRI experiment, Hella Hamid was tasked with remote viewing a power station. During the session, she recorded the perception of steam coming out of a kettle. Ingo Swann found this very interesting, and it led him to a principle concerning how the remote viewer processes psychic information though their own filters and levels of knowledge and understanding.

In the process of objectifying the psychic data, Swann surmised that as Hella's conscious mind had no understanding of how a power station worked, it had associated the mechanism with the nearest thing it could: a boiling kettle.

Later, she visited and toured a power station, and the next time she had one as a target, her session described it in detail.[56]

Compassion

Many religions and philosophies espouse tenets of compassion; they know that, at one level, we are all connected (as in Cayce's 'trumpet of the universe'). Cayce set himself an ideal early in childhood to help others, especially sick children, and was able to do so through his intuitive gift.

Could compassion for all, including oneself, instilling the notion of the connectedness of all within the remote viewer, be another factor in facilitating movement through the levels of consciousness?

Practices such as the Metta (loving kindness) meditation, an ancient practice said to predate Buddhism, could help.

Here, you first mediate on your own peace and happiness:

May I be happy.

May I be well.

May I be safe.

May I be peaceful and at ease.

Then, you wish for the happiness and well-being of others by repeating the phrases below, keeping each of the following in mind, in turn - first a good friend, then a person you feel neutral towards, followed by a person with whom you have some difficulty and, finally, all sentient beings:

May you be happy.

May you be well.

May you be safe.

May you be peaceful and at ease.

A Very Short History of Modern-day Remote Viewing in the United States

The following is a very brief overview of recent remote viewing history to put some of the names mentioned previously into the context of a timeline. Leaving out many key individuals and events - in particular, those related to the latter part of the Star Gate programme, and specifically CRV - it is meant as a high-level introduction. For a more complete picture, books and papers giving a broader view are referred to throughout the text or listed at the end.

'They Defy Logic, But the Facts are Undeniable'

'Psychic helped locate downed U.S. plane, ex-president says', ran a Reuters headline from 21 September 1995.

The story referred to a response that former United States President Jimmy Carter gave to an Emory University student, who had asked if anything unusual had happened during his time in office. Carter explained that a plane, which had crashed under a tree canopy, had gone undetected by satellites and search planes for two weeks after the accident. As reported by Reuters, the ex-president said:

> *I have to say that without my knowledge, the head of the CIA asked her to come in. She went into a trance. And while she was in the trance, she gave some latitude and longitude figures. We focused our satellite cameras on that point and the plane was there.*

He was referring to an event that took place 16 years earlier, in March 1979, in which a Russian Tu-22 spy plane had crashed in Africa. Finding it would be a major intelligence win for the United States.

Gary Langford, a remote viewer at SRI, and a woman working with Dale Graff at the United States Air Force's Foreign Technology Division worked on the task. Provided only with the continent and the type of aircraft, both viewers produced descriptions of a crash area that were found to match the actual location. The woman also drew the flight path and marked the area of the downed plane on a map, which proved to be within three miles of the actual site.[57,58]

Carter noted the subsequent briefing with the CIA on 11 April of that year in his diary, later published as *White House Diary*.

> *CIA briefing.... that a plane had crashed in Zambia. An American parapsychologist had been able to pinpoint the site of the crash. We've had several reports of this parapsychology working; one discovered the map coordinates of a site and accurately described a camouflaged missile test site. Both we and the Soviets use these parapsychologists on occasion to help us with sensitive intelligence matters, and the results are unbelievable.*

Looking back on the subject for the publication of his *White House Diary* Carter wrote:

> *The proven results of these exchanges between our intelligence services and parapsychologists raise some of the most intriguing and unanswerable questions of my presidency. They defy logic, but the facts are undeniable.[59]*

On 28 November 1995, a month after the Reuters' news story, the United States public heard that their government's use of psychics in locating the missing plane was not a one-off occurrence, but part of a systematic endeavour. What was once one of the most secret of government programmes was discussed in the most public of forums: *Nightline,* the national news programme from ABC. It was revealed that the government had funded research and used psychics for operations for 23 years at the cost of $20 million[60] (cheap compared to the amount of money spent on other methods of intelligence gathering[61]). Joining host Ted Koppel were CIA Director Robert Gates, a CIA 'Customer Representative' to the Star Gate programme going by the name of 'Norm' for the evening, and Ed May, head of the research arm of the programme.

Gates stated emphatically that remote viewing made no contribution to policy decision.

'Norm' explained an 'eight-martini' event, an in-house CIA term for information provided by a psychic, which was so on-target and unexpected that the antidote, to regain some semblance of reality, was a heavy drinking session.

Koppel aimed to provide a balanced view, but *Nightline* viewers, hearing about the remote viewing programme for the first time, would have been left with the impression that their government had taken 23 years to realize something didn't worked. There is, however, more to the story...

New Beginnings for Parapsychology

The first experiment to be termed 'remote viewing' had taken place at the American Society for Psychical Research (ASPR) in New York City in December 1971. Ingo Swann, New York artist, was tasked with sensing weather conditions at a *remote* location. Tucson, Arizona was the chosen target: *'The wind is blowing. It's cold. And it is raining hard.'* Feedback was provided by a telephone call to the local weather service. Indeed, Tucson was experiencing an unseasonal thunderstorm with temperatures near freezing.[62]

Later, in February 1972, the first 'outbounder' experiment was performed; an employee of the ASPR visited the nearby Natural History Museum, while Swann, ensconced at the ASPR offices, accurately described the sights and sounds that the outbounder had encountered.

Swann had also worked with Gertrude Schmeidler of the City College of New York, where, in a controlled experiment, he had induced temperature change in thermistors sealed in thermos bottles.

Free Response vs. Forced Choice

These early experiments from the 1970s demonstrate an important shift in parapsychology experimentation from previous decades.

In 1935, Joseph B. Rhine established the Duke Parapsychology Laboratory with the goal of presenting statistical evidence for psi. The effort produced statistically significant results, published in two books: *Extrasensory Perception* in 1934 and *Extrasensory Perception After Sixty Years* in 1940. Today, the findings are dismissed by those who have not studied them, but the control under which the experiments were conducted by Rhine and his team stand as an example of rigorous parapsychological research.

Experiments at the Duke lab were based around specially designed 'Zener' cards: packs of 25 cards, each displaying one of five distinct symbols. (They are still  available for purchase from the Rhine Research Center.) As a test of pre-cognitive abilities, participants, known as 'subjects', would be asked to state the symbol on the next card in the pack. The choice would be recorded and the card moved to a different pile. This would continue until the pack had been completed, at which point the number of correct selections would be recorded.

As a test of telepathy, a subject sitting across the desk from a 'sender' would be asked to state the symbol that the sender was looking at. Having the subject and sender in different rooms, and even different buildings, made no difference to the results.

Experiments where there is a limited set of known of choices, as in the case of Zener cards, where the subject knows that the card must contain one of five symbols, are known as 'forced-choice' experiments. They have the advantage of being easily translated into statistics, as the selection is either a hit or miss. In a run of 25 selections by the subject, five would be expected to be correct by chance.

However, as the task has little meaning and provides no interest for the subject, it becomes boring and produces what is known as a 'decline effect'; over time, subjects see a lessening of the ability to select the correct symbol, as if the psychic mechanism losses interest in the task.

What was significant in the remote viewing experiments from the early 1970s in New York, is that there was no limited and known set of options for the subject to choose from. The participant was allowed a 'free response', that is, they were free to describe whatever the target is. Although harder to set up and more difficult to convert into statistics, free-response experiments are closer to how psi phenomena present themselves 'in the wild'. This type of experimentation became the standard at SRI and no decline effect was seen.

Not that free-response experiments were new; some examples that predate these early Swann trials are described in two books from the 1920's. René Warcollier's *La Télepathie* (published in 1921 and later published in English as *Mind to Mind*) and Upton Sinclair's *Mental Radio* (published in 1929, it included a preface by Albert Einstein, saying it deserved 'most earnest consideration').

Of further significance in the ASPR and Schmeidler experiments, Swann was treated less as a subject to be studied, but as a collaborator with the experimenters. This type of partnership becomes the standard approach at SRI and a trend in other parapsychology research environments.

Swann at SRI

Whilst a teacher at Stanford University in the late 1960s, Dr. Hal Puthoff had co-authored *Fundamentals of Quantum Electronics,* a text book on quantum physics; and, in doing so, realized something was missing from science: 'What about animate life? What about consciousness? Are there additional fields that we just don't know about?'

In searching for answers, he became intrigued by the 'Baxter effect', which he had read about in Ostrander and Schroeder's *Psychic Discoveries Behind the Iron Curtain*. Cleve Baxter, a polygraph expert based in New York, had run a series of experiments measuring plants and cell cultures with polygraph machines, which indicated, for example, that plants reacted to a person's thoughts of harming them.

By 1972, Puthoff had moved into research at the Stanford Research Institute (SRI), where he planned to perform experiments with culture cells along the lines of Baxter's research. He proposed that if a group of cells was split into two, and one set was perturbed, and the other reacted as Baxter had demonstrated, and the two sets were sufficiently far apart, it would be possible to measure the speed of propagation. He wrote up these ideas in the form of a proposal for an experiment and mailed it to Baxter.

Ingo Swann knew Baxter and had taken part in some of his experiments. Through this connection, Swann had seen Puthoff's proposal and found it interesting enough that he wrote to him to suggest he use human subjects instead of cell cultures. He included copies of the write-ups of the experiments with Gertrude Schmeidler and offered his services.

Taking him up on his offer, Puthoff invited Swann to California in June 1972. Shortly after Swann arrived, Puthoff took him to Stanford University's Varian Physics Building. Here Swann was asked to describe a piece of scientific equipment that was hidden from view under the floor. This highly technical instrument, a magnetometer designed to detect magnetic fields, was installed in such a way as to be imperturbable from the outside world, being sealed with electric, magnetic, superconducting and acoustic shielding.

Swann was able to both sketch the device and affect its output,[63] neither of which should have been possible given the fact its design had not been published and the layers of shielding. The experiment was written up and sent to several of Puthoff's contacts, including Dr. 'Kit' Green at the CIA, for their thoughts.

There was, at the time, some concern in the intelligence community of a 'psi gap' with Russia. A paper written by the Medical Intelligence Office of the Defense Intelligence Agency (DIA), entitled *Controlled Offensive Behavior - USSR, July 1972*, warned that the Russians were spending a great deal of money, and effort in various universities, investigating psychic abilities:

> *In summary, what is the strategic threat posed by the current "explosion" in Soviet parapsychological research? Soviet efforts in the field of psi research, sooner or later, might enable them to do some of the following:*
>
> > *a.   Know the contents of top-secret US documents, the movements of our troops and ships and the location and nature of our military installations*
> >
> > *b.   Mold the thoughts of key US military and civilian leaders, at a distance*

c. *Cause the instant death of any United States official, at a distance*

d. *Disable, at a distance, US military equipment of all types including space craft*

Many in the intelligence community did not believe any of it: 'The greatest threat was that they would stop wasting money on this!'[64] But, the CIA, in doing its job to investigate possible threats, needed someone to research the limits of psi abilities and confirm that the Russians were indeed just wasting their time. Hal Puthoff and SRI were the logical choice. SRI was already a major government contractor, and Puthoff had the necessary qualifications, security clearances and as shown by the magnetometer paper, interest in the area of concern. Further experiments were arranged with Swann that required him to describe a range of small items hidden in boxes. Swann did well enough to show that there was something to be studied, and so in October 1972, a $50,000 eight-month contract was signed.

In April 1973, NASA signed a contract with SRI based on a proposal entitled 'Development of Techniques to Enhance Man/Machine Communication' after Russell Targ had demonstrated the ESP training machine (today an iPhone app) he had developed to James Fletcher, the director of the organization, Wernher von Braun and Edgar Mitchell.[65]

And so started the 23-year-long, government-funded programme to understand the applications and boundaries of psychic functioning.

New Experiments: Outbounders and Project SCANATE

Describing 'what's in the box-type' experiments as a trivialization of his talents (declaring 'if you want to know what's inside the box, open the lid'), Swann suggested the outbounder protocol, used previously at the ASPR, as a more interesting task.

Through a series of refinements, the procedure evolved to guard against the possibility of fraud: random target selection from a previously defined target pool of numbered envelopes containing locations within driving distance, created by someone otherwise not involved in the project. These were stored in a safe controlled by someone otherwise not involved in the project. Blindness of both the target pool and the selected target was ensured for the viewer and monitor, while the outbounder was only allowed to open the envelope to discover the location they should travel to, once they were outside the building. After several trials had been run the typed session transcripts were given, along with the list of locations that the outbounder had visited, to a judge, who was otherwise not involved in the project. The judge's role was to visit each place and classify the transcripts in order of best match to the location. The resulting rank order would then be used to produce statistics.

In April 1973, Swann suggested a new experiment. On the premise that an outbounder was not necessary - there was no need for an information 'sender' to be on-site at the target location for the process to work - Swann proposed targeting locations by their geographic coordinates. Initially sceptical, Puthoff and Targ agreed to set up test targets using the coordinate method. This became known as Project SCANATE, a compounding of '*scan*ning by coordin*ate*', a name Swann thought the CIA might like.

After a number of trial runs, Puthoff contacted Dr. Green at the CIA to say that they were running a new experiment and ask if Green could supply geographic coordinates of a location that he knew of, they could use as a test. Puthoff wanted to remove himself from the site selection, as did Green, who asked a colleague if he knew of a location. Coordinates were passed to Puthoff and the remote viewing took place. Both Swann and Pat Price provided sessions that described a well-maintained military-type installation. Swann drew a series of buildings and boundaries. Both viewers indicated an underground area. Price went onto describe storage rooms, military personnel and equipment, as well as the titles of papers on desks ('Flytrap' and 'Minerva') and labels from folders locked in a file cabinet ('Cueball', '14 Ball', '8 Ball', '4 Ball' and 'Rackup').[66]

The actual coordinates were for Green's colleague's summer cabin in the Blue Ridge Mountains of West Virginia, and the experiment was judged to be a failure, a major disappointment for SRI team. However, very close to the cabin was Sugar Grove Station, a top-secret National Security Agency (NSA) centre. In regard to that location much of the information was correct; Swann's map of the buildings proved to be accurate in terms of location and relative distance, while Price's list of words turned out to be code names associated with the installation.

The infiltration of the NSA facility rang alarms bells at the CIA and, presuming a serious security breach an aggressively thorough investigation of all involved ensued. However, it also resulted in continued funding for the programme and the request that a foreign target of interest be selected for the next experiment.

Writing an article for an internal CIA magazine in 1977 (later released to the public in 1996), *Parapsychology in Intelligence: A Personal Review and Conclusions*, Dr. Kenneth A. Kress, CIA project officer for the SRI work, recalled that, in February 1974:

> The project proceeded on the premise that the phenomena existed; the objective was to develop and utilize them.

Research was to proceed along two lines:

1. *identification of measurable physiological or psychological characteristics of psychic individuals, and the establishment of experimental protocols for validating paranormal abilities.*

2. *operational utility of psychic subjects without regard to the detailed understanding of paranormal functioning.*[67]

In July 1974, a target of interest was selected: Semipalatinsk in the USSR, an industrial complex that the CIA had limited knowledge of. Price, working from the geographic coordinates, described a massive, two to three-story gantry crane on rails, a series of buildings and some large gas cylinders. From satellite imagery, these elements were known to be at the site; and so, with this validation, he was asked to describe the buildings and activities taking place within them. Over several days, a mass of notes and sketches was made as Price investigated each of the buildings. In one, he perceived the construction of a large sphere, 60-ft in diameter and made from metal segments that had been welded together.

Typical of the sort of response this type of work was getting within the intelligence community, two analyst groups refused to look at the data: one because it was 'unscientific nonsense', and the other because it could be 'demonic'.

Eventually, an analyst group was found, and much of the layout of the location was verified by the information provided by satellite imagery, but the description of what was happening within the buildings was not. A few years later, in May 1977, the existence of the large sphere was verified, again by satellite imagery, as it was seen outside the building. Sadly, Price never heard this final piece of validating feedback as he had died two years earlier.[68]

As for the 'identification of measurable physiological or psychological characteristics of psychic individuals', SRI remote viewers were put though a barrage of medical, neuropsychological and psychological profiling tests.[69] After all the testing, it turned out they were just 'normal people', so the next step was to identify some 'normal people', self-professed non-psychics to see if they could produce results. Volunteers were found from around SRI as control subjects, including Targ's friend, Hella Hamid. A series of outbounder experiments were run as a comparison between the psychics and the new 'non-psychic' recruits. Hamid proved to be an excellent remote reviewer and went onto work with Stephan Schwartz on his archaeological projects.

Published Studies

Explaining to the CIA that having two laser-physicists working at SRI and *not* publishing papers would attract more attention for their top-secret programme than allowing them to do so, Targ and Puthoff were permitted to publish some of their findings in scientific journals, without disclosing who was funding them.

In October 1974, their first paper, *Information Transmission Under Conditions of Sensory Shielding,* was published in the prestigious science journal, *Nature*. The paper discusses several series of experiments: in one, Uri Gellar was tasked with reproducing previously drawn pictures; another involved a series of outbounder experiments with Pat Price; and the final experiments were tests to measure a subject's perception to a flashing light presented to another person, in another room.

Their conclusions were:

- *A channel exists whereby information about a remote location can be obtained by means of an as yet unidentified perceptual modality.*

- *As with all biological systems, the information channel appears to be imperfect, containing noise along with the signal.*

- *While a quantitative signal-to-noise ratio in the information theoretical sense cannot as yet be determined, the results of our experiments indicate that the functioning is at the level of useful information transfer.*

It may be that remote perceptual ability is widely distributed in the general population, but because the perception is generally below an individual's level of awareness, it is repressed or not noticed.

Our observation of the phenomena leads us to conclude that experiments in the area of so-called paranormal phenomena can be scientifically conducted, and it is our hope that other laboratories will initiate additional research to attempt to replicate these findings.

In March 1976, *A Perceptual Channel for Information Transfer Over Kilometer Distances: Historical Perspective and Recent Research was published* in the *Proceedings of the IEEE*. The paper discusses further outbounder experiments comparing 'experienced' to 'learner' subjects.

In 1977, the book *Mind-Reach: Scientists Look at Psychic Abilities* detailed the experiments performed and the scientists' thoughts on what they were seeing. 1979 saw the publication, with Ed May, of *Direct Perception of Remote Geographical Locations*, presented at the American Association for the Advancement of Science. Written three years after *Mind Reach*, the paper discusses findings since the book's publication. Made available as an appendix to the Hampton Roads 2005 edition of the book, the paper's introduction sees the authors now comfortable talking about 'non-local direct perception' and 'Remote viewing's independence of space and time'.

> ...by the time we were seven years into the program it was clear to us that remote viewing accuracy and reliability were not sensitive functions of either distance or time.

Independent Replication

These published materials caught the imagination of several individuals who sought to replicate the tests for themselves. The first of these was John Bisaha, a psychology professor at Chicago's Mundelein College, who, with student Brenda Dunne, performed a series of outbounder experiments following the SRI outbounder model. These were published in *Research in Parapsychology* in 1976 as *Precognitive Remote Viewing in the Chicago Area: A Replication of the Stanford Experiment*.

Many such replications have since been performed. In 1982, a catalogue of outbounder-type experiments was collated by George Hansen, Marilyn Schlitz and Charles Tart, who found that:

> ...more than half (fifteen out of 28) of the published formal experiments have been successful, where only one in twenty would be expected by chance. We have also located eighteen unpublished studies, with eight reporting statistical significance; thus the success of remote viewing is not due to reporting bias, in which vast numbers of unsuccessful experiments go unreported.[70]

Princeton Engineering Anomalies Research

Brenda Dunne later joined Professor Robert Jahn, Dean of the School of Engineering and Applied Science at Princeton University, and together they started the Princeton Engineering Anomalies Research Lab, (the PEAR lab) in 1979. As well as numerous psychokinesis experiments with various mechanical and electronic random number generators, over 650 remote viewing trials were run until the lab closed when Jahn retired in 2007. Remote viewing at PEAR was called 'precognitive remote perception' and its viewers known as 'percipients', whilst the outbounder was the 'agent'.

After a successful replication of the SRI outbounder trials, with standard best-place matching by independent human judges, PEAR looked to obtain more concise statistics by replacing the human judge with codified percipient responses in the form of a 30-question questionnaire; for example: Question 4, 'From the agent's perspective, is the scene well bounded, such as the interior of a room, a stadium, or a courtyard?', or Question 29, 'Is water a significant part of the scene?'. Each response could be marked as either correct or incorrect, the thinking being that this would be more accurate than the subjective ability of a judge to make a match between the session transcript and the location.

This strategy produced a decline in significance from the earlier free-response trials. Assuming the problem was that the single binary response was too restrictive, a four-point scale was introduced to allow the percipient to state whether the feature was present (4), present but not dominant (3), uncertainty as to the existence of the feature (2), and that the feature was not present (1).

A further decline in significance was seen. Assuming the percipient was still too restricted in their responses, a 10-point, 0-9 scale system was implemented to allow the percipient to give weight to those elements that they felt more strongly at the site. Again, this approach saw an even greater decline in significance to chance.

It seemed that as the level of analysis increased, the effect diminished. The questionnaire seemed to impose a limiting structure in the mind of the viewer, moving the session more towards a forced-choice exercise as opposed to one of free response. Despite this, the overall results of the PEAR studies are still highly significant (33 million to one against chance).[71]

Stephan Schwartz and the Mobius Society

Independent from Targ and Puthoff's work, Stephan Schwartz had identified and codified processes and protocols similar to those developed at SRI, after having studied the Edgar Cayce readings and associated materials. In 1977, he founded the Mobius Society to further the exploration and application of anomalous cognition.

Schwartz saw archaeology as an excellent practical test of remote viewing's capabilities: describe something lost to time and its location, find it, and then compare the archaeology to the information received psychically.

One of the new organization's first projects was a collaboration with the SRI team, namely, May, Targ and Puthoff, along with remote viewers Swann and Hammid. Schwartz had arranged time on a mini-submarine and had a number of experiments planned, under a project he called 'Deep Quest'.

From previous experimentation most of the electromagnetic (EM) spectrum had been ruled out as being the mechanism that facilitated anomalous perception. For example, studies at SRI found that remote viewing from within a Faraday cage did not diminish the effect; in fact, some viewers preferred it. The final piece of the EM spectrum, extreme low frequencies (ELFs), could be shielded by a depth of seawater. If remote viewing was possible in such depths, it would prove it was not a function of information transference through the EM spectrum. A pool of outbounder locations was prepared as targets for these experiments.

As a second component of Deep Quest Schwartz assigned a simple message to each target in the pool of outbounder locations. Taking inspiration from Admiral Nelson's use of signal flags to issue commands to his fleet, Schwartz proposed that pre-defined messages could be conveyed through the ability of a psychic to describe the target associated to the message.

The third component of Deep Quest was archaeological. Prior to the dive, five viewers were asked to identify areas of interest on a sea chart of the area and describe items that they thought would be found, and the circumstances of how they got there. 'Out of the area of more than 1,500 square miles, all five picked the same area of about 180 square yards.'[72] A previously unknown wreck, as described by the remote viewers, was found, and much of the information they predicted aligned with what was known of the ship after its history had been researched.

The remote viewing of the outbounder location targets from inside the submarine, at depths of hundreds of feet of seawater, one each by Swann and Hammid, were successful, ruling out ELFs as the mechanism for data transfer. The messages associated with these targets were delivered, the first use of ARV.

A later Mobius project was a large-scale expedition to Alexandria, Egypt. Schwartz' consensus protocol was used to tag each piece of information provided by 11 remote viewers. These tags were then combined to create 'concepts'. As with Deep Quest, each viewer had been given a map of the area and asked to mark areas of archaeological interest. The information was analysed and consolidated to maps that were to be used on-site. Psychics Hella Hammid and George McMullen joined Schwartz in Egypt. The expedition uncovered Cleopatra's Palace and Mark Anthony's Timonium, as well as other sites. Of the close-to-10,000 concepts that could be tested, 78% were assessed by archaeologists as being correct, with a further 10% assessed as partially correct.[73]

Both the Deep Quest and Alexandria expeditions were filmed, and some video is available online. Schwartz has published several papers on aspects of anomalous cognition including further archaeological projects using remote viewing.

Project Star Gate

Lieutenant 'Skip' Atwater was part of the Systems Exploitation Detachment of the United States Army's Intelligence and Security Command (INSCOM), tasked with the operational security of military installations - evaluating a base's readiness against security breaches. During one such evaluation in 1977 his team was presented with Puthoff and Targ's *Mind-Reach* and the question, '...how are we supposed to protect ourselves from *this*?'.[74]

Atwater knew the only way to find out was to put remote viewing to the test. Due to the clearances required, it had to be done with resources internal to the army. After a recruitment exercise six army personnel, including Joe McMoneagle, were selected from a pool of 30 candidates with the help of Targ and Puthoff.

The six were sent to SRI in May 1979 for further evaluation and training. Each of them carried out six outbounder trials, giving 36 sessions in total. Their results were statistically significant, in that they produced 19 first-place matches where six would be expected by chance.[75]

The army unit established at Fort Meade, Maryland, was known by several names during its lifetime, including Gondola Wish, Grill Flame, Center Lane, Dragoon Absorb and Sun Streak. Star Gate, its final name, is now commonly used to refer to the combined programme of military operational and research efforts.

As a test of the threat assessment (if we can do it, someone else could) that Atwater saw as a risk, McMoneagle was tasked with describing a secret piece of advanced military technology: the M1 Abrams tank. McMoneagle was able to draw a cross-sectional schematic, and describe many aspects of the innovative design, including its computer-aided, laser-targeting system and the gun assembly.

In November 1979, the Iran hostage crisis plunged the group into operations mode, as they were tasked with monitoring the health of the hostages, their surroundings and captors in detail on a daily basis for over a year.[76]

Another example, often recounted,[77] again by McMoneagle, is the remote viewing of the 'Typhoon' submarine at Severodvinsk Shipyard 402 in the USSR. Notable not only for its exemplary remote viewing, but also for the response it received. Activities at the shipyard were a matter of intense speculation within navy and security circles. Satellite imagery showed a mass of materials entering a massive building, but what was happening inside?

Tasked by being shown an overhead image of the roof of a large building, McMoneagle went onto describe the activities taking place inside, eventually sensing a 'very large submarine', with missile tubes in front of the conning tower and an unconventional shape at the front and stern.

The findings were unexpected; they ran contrary to typical submarine construction and, given the unconventional source of the information they were largely ignored. Asked when the 'submarine' would be launched, McMoneagle viewed the site again and noted the difference in the state of construction. He estimated the completion date to be in four months' time. Four months later, in mid-January 1980, a very large submarine, the largest ever built, much as McMoneagle had described, was seen moored in the Severodvinsk Shipyard. It represented a formidable threat to the balance of power and, apparently, a big surprise to many on the National Security Council who had ignored the remote viewing data, one of whom was Robert Gates, later to became director of the CIA, and later still to appear on *Nightline* to state that remote viewing was not useful as an intelligence gathering tool.

Building on their prior research, Swann and Puthoff had formalized a more structured approach to remote viewing, which they felt could be more easily taught. Swann called it 'coordinate remote viewing' after his geographic targeting system, but later renamed it 'controlled remote viewing' to emphasize the structured approach. The first two army personnel were trained in this new method in 1983, while a second group of six, including Paul H. Smith and Ed Dames, were trained in 1984. Those trained developed their own *Coordinate Remote Viewing Training Manual*, referred to earlier, which was subsequently used as part of the training materials for other members of the military group, including Lyn Buchanan and David Morehouse.

What is now known as the HRVG methodology was developed in the early 1980s by United States Army Special Forces working with noted psychic Dr. Richard Ireland.

In 1982, Targ, along with SRI consultant, Keith Harary, with financial investors, started Delphi Consultants, an organisation designed to put psychic abilities to work commercially. At the end of the year, the organization made the front page of *The Wall Street Journal* due to its use of ARV to produce a row of nine successful forecasts of the silver futures market, seven of which were traded, resulting in a profit of $120,000.[78,79]

By 1985, Puthoff had left the SRI research programme, and Ed May, who had joined the team in 1975, became the director. In 1991, May secured new funding and a new home for the research effort at SAIC.

Star Gate Closure: Remote Viewing Goes Public

On 29 September 1995, the American Institutes for Research (AIR) published its study, *An Evaluation of Remote Viewing: Research and Applications*. AIR had been tasked by the CIA to review the research and 'operational application of the remote viewing phenomenon in intelligence gathering'.

The Research Evaluation section of the report stated:

> *A statistically significant laboratory effort has been demonstrated in the sense that hits occur more often than chance.*

Jessica Utts, quoted earlier, stated in the Conclusions and Recommendations section of the report:

> *It is clear to this author that anomalous cognition is possible and has been demonstrated. This conclusion is not based on belief, but rather on commonly accepted scientific criteria.[80]*

Dr. Ray Hyman, a psychologist from the University of Oregon and a prominent sceptic, was also tasked with evaluating the materials for the AIR report. Although he admitted an effect, he disagreed with Utts' conclusions that psychic functioning was the explanation. That said, he could not offer an alternative:

> *I will grant them that they have apparently demonstrated that the SAIC and the ganzfeld experiments have generated significant effect sizes beyond what we should expect from chance variations. I will further admit that, at this writing, I cannot suggest obvious methodological flaws to account for these significant effects. As I have previously mentioned, this admission does not mean that these experiments are free from subtle biases and potential bugs. The experimental paradigms are too recent and insufficiently evaluated to know for sure.[81]*

As the goal of the AIR report was to evaluate 'all laboratory experiments and meta-analytic reviews conducted as part of the research program', the admission that the work was 'insufficiently evaluated' is surprising.

Less surprising, that as a professional denier, despite the evidence, he cannot admit that there is any psychic explanation. Instead he holds the line for scientism, hoping that, if we wait long enough, flaws in the experiments can be found.

It seems that, unlike Utts, Hyman's conclusion is based on belief, rather than on commonly accepted scientific criteria.

More damming was the report's operational evaluation:

> In no case had the information provided ever been used to guide intelligence operations. Thus, remote viewing failed to produce actionable intelligence.

The findings of the AIR study are strongly repudiated by Ed May,[82] and Paul H. Smith, who cite flaws in the methods and scope of the evaluation.

As May points out, the study did not seek input from clients of the programme, namely, the many governmental agencies, [83] including the CIA, NASA, DARPA and DIA, as well as the United States Army INSCOM, Navy and Airforce, that had repeatedly used the services of the remote viewers over the years.

Dr. Smith's four-part essay, *A Review of the A.I.R. Report*, states that only a year's worth of data was used, selected from when the programme was poorly managed, the viewers were demoralized, and the tried-and-trusted CRV and ERV procedures were no longer the principle acquisition methods.[84] The study reviewed a faction of the work the programme provided (only the last 10 experiments of the hundreds performed over the years), and discounted the 3,000 to 4,000 operational remote viewing sessions from prior to 1994.[85]

More telling is the fact the CIA had ordered the combined research and army programme to close the previous June, three months before the study had been concluded. This timing and the scope taken by researchers in making their evaluation point to a foregone conclusion.

With remote viewing out in the open following the programme's closure, several of the ex-military viewers wrote books, and started their own remote viewing training and operational service companies. Students of these have now started their own companies.

Glenn Wheaton started the HRVG in 1995, as:

> a skill-based association of people interested in the Research and Development of Remote Viewing. The Guild, without

prejudice, examines, studies, and evaluates Remote Viewing methodologies from the various schools of instruction. We intend to make every effort to understand the process of Remote Viewing as well as its application as a tool regarding targets of interest to the Guild.[86]

Visitors come from all over the world to be trained in the HRVG method. They have also been visited by film crews from Japan and Korea. HRVG, normally represented by Wheaton himself, regularly presents at IRVA meetings.

In 1999 IRVA was formed by many of those mentioned above, as stated on its website:

> *The mission of the International Remote Viewing Association is to provide historic, scientific, and educational material and support to the remote viewing community and general public on the subject of Remote Viewing.*
>
> *IRVA's primary goal is to provide an unbiased approach relative to information, testing, research and education regarding Remote Viewing.*[87]

To these ends IRVA produces a magazine, *Aperture*, and holds conferences most years, while members have access to a video library of past conferences.

Dunne and Jahn from the PEAR lab established the International Consciousness Research Laboratories to continue their work, while Ed May established the Cognitive Sciences Laboratory at the Laboratories for Fundamental Research, where his research continues.

Today, there is a growing online community of viewers learning, practising, and taking part in projects, in particular, those using ARV to predict the outcomes of sports and financial markets. The Applied Precognition Project (APP) is the core group in this area, it's mission to 'publicly explore, research and apply logic and intuition/emotion to predict future event outcomes, enabling participants to evolve personally while contributing to the elevation of global consciousness'.[88] The organisation is active in supporting ARV groups by running workshops, and holding regular conferences in the United States, with noted speakers on consciousness and remote viewing.

Joe McMoneagle teaches a remote viewing course at the Monroe Institute in Virginia, and Stephan Schwartz regularly teaches his online remote viewing course, 'Opening to the Infinite'.

The Future for Remote Viewing

As Utts said in 1995,

> There is little benefit to continuing experiments designed to offer proof, since there is little more to be offered to anyone who does not accept the current collection of data.[89]

Further remote viewing experimentation should be geared towards understanding what improves its efficacy, whilst the tool itself should be used as designed; to answer questions and investigate the powers of the human consciousness.

Many of the original military remote viewers and some of their students offer such services commercially to businesses and individuals. These include the IRIS organization in France, and the Husick Group in the United States, both of which are setting an exemplary example of how intuition can be integrated with our common approaches to solving problems, creating solutions and pursuing innovation.

The Husick Group, formed by Gail Husick, provides high-quality consensus remote viewing with Husick herself taking on tasking, analysis and project management activities, as well as managing a group of freelance remote viewers. Various projects have been undertaken, from crime to business innovation.

Alexis Champion's IRIS group has been running for 10 years and, although still relatively small, is seeing large year-on-year growth. The company has two components: teaching and business consultancy. The business consultancy arm has taken on crime investigation, business innovation, and archaeological projects.

Champion's approach is to make remote viewing appear as a normal, everyday ability by specifically not talking about 'remote viewing'. There is little mention of it on the IRIS website, and meetings with clients do not delve into the history of remote viewing or its published results. For some projects the client is encouraged to be involved and their own staff are taken through a remote viewing style procedure, though approached more as an exercise in meditation and creative visualization.

Unlike some countries where the predominant sceptical view of anything psi hinders its acceptance as a viable source, Champion has an advantage in that corporate France views results as being more important than how they were produced. IRIS has received national television coverage more than once and count as their clients many of Europe's largest organizations from areas as diverse and conservative as banking and travel.

Whilst these new companies, and others are offering quality remote viewing based services for paying customers, there is a large group of individuals and small groups working on various projects. The *eight martinis* magazine, produced by Daz Smith, is a great resource on all things 'remote viewing', including examples of its application:

- Crime:
    - 'Remote Viewing ARSON' by Sandra Hilleard (issue 2 July 2009),
- Helping to find missing people:
    - 'The Missing' by Kelly Snyder and Daz Smith (issue 2 July 2009), and
    - 'Searching....', Daz Smith (issue 3 March 2010),
    - 'Step out of the Box', an account of a humanitarian project run by Angela Thompson Smith (issue 10 November 2013),
- Researching technology failure:
    - '18 Years of Excitement CRV Stories from a Professional Remote Viewer' by Lori Williams (issue 14 April 2016)

- Mysteries:
  - 'Amelia - Remote Viewing Search for Amelia Earhart, Fred Noonan and the Electra', Angela Thompson Smith (issue 9 April 2013),
  - 'What Was That Thing in the Sky Over Oakland California in November 1896?' by Jon Knowles (issue 7 May 2012),
  - 'Fatima, Remote Viewing and the ESP Connection' by Tunde Atunrase (issue 6 January 2012), and
  - 'Remote Viewing Japan Air Line flight 1628 & a UFO Encounter Over Alaska' article also by Tunde Atunrase with remote viewing sessions by Joe McMoneagle (issue 12 January 2015).
- And, of course, remote viewing for fun and profit:
  - 'Remote Viewing Outcomes for Fun and Profit or How to be a Zen monk while in Las Vegas' by Dr. Don Walker (issue 9 April 2013).

Further Materials

Of the mass of Star Gate material produced within SRI, SAIC and the military unit during the 23 years of the programme's existence, 90,000 pages have been declassified, and are available online with an estimated fifth left to be declassified. Ed May and his colleague Sonali Bhatt Marwaha are compiling and editing the material for publication in four volumes as *The Star Gate Archives, Reports of the United States Government Sponsored Psi Program, 1972-1995.*

Many remote viewing related published papers are available from IRVA's online library at: www.irva.org/library/articles/

There are a number of insightful renderings of the early days of remote viewing in the United States, available for free online:

- Stephan Schwartz' excellent overview of the modern remote viewing period: Through Time and Space: The Evidence for Remote Viewing is especially interesting as an outline of his own work and his views on Hyman's position

- Schwartz' entry on 'Remote Viewing' in the Society for Psychical Research's *Psi Encyclopedia* can be found at: psi-encyclopedia.spr.ac.uk

- *Anomalous Human Cognition: A Possible Role within the Crucible of Intelligence Collection* (2010) by Douglas Morris

- *Unconventional Human Intelligence Support: Transcendent and Asymmetric Warfare Implications of Remote Viewing* (2001) by Commander L. R. Bremseth of the United States Navy

- *CIA-initiated Remote Viewing Program at Stanford Research Institute* (1996) by Hal Puthoff

- *Remote Viewing at Stanford Research Institute in the 1970s: A Memoir* (1996) by Russell Targ

- *Parapsychology in Intelligence: A Personal Review and Conclusions, Studies in Intelligence* (1977) by Dr. Kenneth A. Kress

Recommended Books and Websites

Books

There are many books available on remote viewing. Anything by Joe McMoneagle, Russell Targ, and Stephan Schwartz are highly recommended. The following incomplete list are highlights that I have enjoyed and feel give a good background to remote viewing history, methodologies, and capabilities.

Russell Targ and Harold Puthoff
Mind-Reach: Scientists Look at Psychic Abilities
Describes the early days at SRI, including the magnetometer experiment, and the testing methodologies employed.

Russell Targ
Limitless Mind - a guide to remote viewing and transformation of consciousness
The Reality of ESP - A Physicist's Proof of Psychic Abilities

Russell Targ and Keith Harary
The Mind Race: Understanding and Using Psychic Abilities

Stephan Schwartz
Opening to the Infinite
The Secret Vaults of Time - Psychic Archaeology and the Quest for Man's Beginnings

Jim Schnabel
Remote Viewers: The Secret History of America's Psychic Spies
Comprehensive overview of the United States government's history with remote viewing from the SRI beginnings and the creation of the protocols, through to the Army's involvement, and eventual disbandment.

Dr. Paul H. Smith
Reading the Enemy's Mind: Inside Star Gate: America's Psychic Espionage Program
Another excellent overview of the Star Gate program. Includes a comprehensive overview of the CRV methodology, and Paul's experience of being trained by Ingo Swann.

The Essential Guide to Remote Viewing
Review of the modern-day remote viewing history, the methodologies and opportunities for learning remote viewing.

Joe McMoneagle
Remote Viewing Secrets
The Stargate Chronicles - Memoirs of a Psychic Spy

F. Holmes Atwater
Captain of My Ship, Master of My Soul

Also, highly recommended; the *eight martinis* **Remote Viewing magazine** is available for free online from
www.eightmartinis.com

Remote Viewing Related

Elizabeth Lloyd Mayer
Extraordinary Knowing

Michael Talbot
The Holographic Universe

Websites

There's a continually growing list of websites related to remote reviewing, below I have listed some I have found useful. For your convenience, these, and others are linked to from the Resource Library section of www.NaturalRemoteViewing.com

A 'one-stop-shop' list is Jon Knowles' comprehensive 'ONE20+' site. Sites are grouped by topics such as example sessions and sites that have practise targets: www.mprv.net/one20.html

Sites with Practice Targets

www.NaturalRemoteViewing.com

www.rvtargets.com

www.remoteviewed.com/target

www.dojopsi.com/tkr (viewer Studios, Go View!)

www.debrakatz.com/remote-viewing-target-practice

www.aestheticimpact.com/crv/practice-targets.html

Remote Viewing Organizations and People

International Remote Viewing Association (IRVA) - www.irva.org

Stephan Schwartz - www.stephanaschwartz.com

Russell Targ - www.espresearch.com

Dale Graff - dalegraff.com

Ed May Laboratories of Fundamental Research - www.lfr.org

Princeton Engineering Anomalies Research (Pear) - www.princeton.edu/~pear/

Joseph McMoneagle - mceagle.com/category/joe-and-remote-viewing/

Ingo Swann - ingoswann.com

Pam Coronado - www.pamcoronado.com

Christopher Barbour facebook.com/psychicdetectivebarbour

Dr. Paul H. Smith - www.rviewer.com

Daz Smith - www.remoteviewed.com www.remoteviewed.com/remote_viewing_manuals.htm for a selection of manuals including the DIA's Coordinate Remote Viewing Training Manual

Hawaii Remote Viewers' Guild - www.hrvg.org

ARV 4 FUN - arv4fun.com

1ARV - www.1arv.com

Applied Precognition Project (APP) - www.appliedprecog.com

TKR Forum - www.dojopsi.info/forum/index.php

Facebook remote viewing group -
www.facebook.com/groups/remoteviewingadmin/

Husick Group - www.husickgroup.com

IRIS - www.iris-ic.com

Igor Grgić's ARV Studio - www.arv-studio.com

GameDay Psychic - www.gamedaypsychic.com

Other websites of interest

Not directly remote viewing related but relevant to the larger discussion on consciousness and psi abilities:

Society for Psychical Research's Psi
Encyclopedia - psi-encyclopedia.spr.ac.uk

Drawing on the Right Side of the Brain - The Official Website of Betty Edwards - drawright.com

Edgar Cayce A.R.E. - www.edgarcayce.org

Dean Radin - www.deanradin.org

Iain McGilchrist - iainmcgilchrist.com

The Institute of Noetic Sciences - www.noetic.org

Mediation related

Heart Math Institute - www.heartmath.com and
www.heartmath.org

Monroe Institute - www.monroeinstitute.org

IONS Institute of Noetic Sciences -

www.noetic.org/meditation-bibliography

Relaxation Response - www.relaxationresponse.org

ziva meditation - zivameditation.com

Headspace - www.headspace.com

www.NaturalRemoteViewing.com

www.facebook.com/groups/NRVBook/

NaturalRemoteViewing@gmail.com

End Notes

[1] '"Psi" is now generally used to denote the psychic functions of telepathy, clairvoyance, precognition and psychokinesis.' Psi Encyclopedia (psi-encyclopedia.spr.ac.uk).

[2] 'The experimental paradigms are too recent and insufficiently evaluated to know for sure.' Dr. Ray Hyman, *An Evaluation of Remote Viewing*.

[3] (May, Utts and Trask, Review of The Psychoenergetic Research Conducted at SRI International (1973-1988) 1989).

[4] (Dunne and Jahn, Information and Uncertainty in Remote Perception Research 2003).

[5] (Storm, Tressoldi and Di Risio 2010).

[6] (Gurney, Myers and Podmore 1886).

[7] Cox (1956) Precognition: An Analysis II. *Journal of the American Society for Psychical Research*, 30, 99-109. Cox conducted an analysis of ticket sales during the period of 28 train crashes between 1950 and 1955 and found the number of tickets sold on the days on which the crashes took place was lower than on other days.

[8] (Dean, 1974).

[9] As quoted in *The Coordinate Remote Viewing Manual*, P. H. Smith, et al, based on language used in prior SRI documents, i.e. Puthoff and Targ, *Perceptual Augemnetation Techniques* 1975.

[10] Paul H. Smith covers the variants of CRV, and well as other remote methods, and gives his thoughts and recommendations on learning remote viewing in his *The Essential Guide to Remote Viewing*.

[11] (Puthoff, RV Reliability, Enhancement, and Evaluation 1984, 10)

[12] (Ullman, Krippner and Vaughan 1989).

[13] (Sherwood and Roe 2003).

[14] (Radin, Entangled Minds 2006, 109-110).

[15] (Graff, Explorations in Precognitive Dreaming 2007).

[16] (Graff and Cyrus, Perceiving the future news: Evidence for retrocausation 2017).

[17] 'ARV' is described later in the section 'The Uses of Remote Viewing'.

[18] email exchange with Nancy Smith.

[19] (May, Utts and Trask, Review of The Psychoenergetic Research Conducted at SRI International (1973-1988) 1989).

[20] Listed as the bibliography (Hansen, Schlitz and Tart 1984, 265).

[21] (Utts 1996, 2)

[22] (Puthoff and Targ, A Perceptual Channel for Information Transfer Over

Kilometer Distances: Historical Perspective and Recent Research 1976).

[23] (Puthoff, Targ and May, Direct perception of remote geographic locations 1979).

[24] (Schlitz and Gruber, Transcontinental Remote Viewing 1980).

[25] Ingo Swann recounts the story of the remote viewing and gives a point-by-point comparison between the remote viewing data and published scientific information in an article written December 1995, *The 1973 Remote Viewing Probe of the Planet Jupiter* republished in eight martinis issue 4 (August 2010).

[26] (Puthoff and Targ, Mind-Reach: Scientists Look at Psychic Abilities 2005, 211).

[27] (Targ, The Reality of ESP 2012, 73).

[28] (Katz, Beem and Fedley, Explorations into Remote Viewing Microscopic Organisms ("The Phage") and the Effects of Biological Scientists' Exposure to Non Local Perception within a Multidisciplinary Approach 2017, 58).

[29] (Kress 1977).

[30] (Puthoff, Keynote speech IRVA Conference 2015).

[31] (Puthoff, Keynote speech IRVA Conference 2015).

[32] (Puthoff, Targ and Humphrey, et al. 1980).

[33] (Schlitz and Honorton, A ganzfeld ESP study within an artistically gifted population 1992).

[34] (Puthoff and Targ, A Perceptual Channel for Information Transfer Over Kilometer Distances: Historical Perspective and Recent Research 1976, Conclusion).

[35] (Schwartz & De Matte, 1982).

[36] (D. Radin 2004).

[37] (McCraty, Atkinson and Bradley, Electrophysiological Evidence of Intuition: Part 2. A System-Wide Process? 2004).

[38] (Palmer 2017) As well as experiment behaviour, an experimenter psi hypothesis has been examined, though results are mixed.

[39] Dean Radin's book, *Supernormal* looks at each of the siddhis in turn and compares the historical record to modern experimentation.

[40] Various studies (Roney-Dougal and Solfvin, Yogic attainment in relation to awareness of precognitive targets 2006), (Roney-Dougal and Solfvin, Exploring the relationship between Tibetan meditation attainment and precognition 2011), (Roney-Dougal, Solfvin and Fox 2008)

[41] (HeartMath Science and Research n.d.)

[42] (Puthoff and Targ, A Perceptual Channel for Information Transfer Over Kilometer Distances: Historical Perspective and Recent Research 1976).

[43] (Swann, The Emergence of Project "Scanate" 1995)

[44] (Puthoff and Targ, Mind-Reach: Scientists Look at Psychic Abilities 2005, 75).

[45] (Watt, 1988).

[46] (Targ, Limitless Mind 2004, 116).

[47] 0-7 Point Evaluation Scale for Target / Transcript Correspondence (Puthoff, Targ and Humphrey, et al. 1980, 27)

[48] (Katz, Grgić and Fendley, An Ethnographical Assessment of Project Firefly: A Yearlong Endeavor to Create Wealth by Predicting FOREX Currency Moves with Associative Remote Viewing 2018)

[49] (Targ, Limitless Mind 2004, 106).

[50] (Targ, Limitless Mind 2004, 116).

[51] (Roser and Gazzaniga 2007).

[52] (Cayce and Cayce 2004, 24)

[53] (Storm and Tressoldi, Gathering in more sheep and goats: A meta-analysis of forced choice sheep-goat ESP studies, 1994-2015 2017)

[54] (Lawrence 1993)

[55] (Walsh 2007)

[56] (Swann, Remote Viewing Processes and Layers of Meaning 2002)

[57] (Graff, Tracks in the Psychic Wilderness, 1998, p. 11).

[58] (Targ, Do You See What I See? 2008, 155)

[59] (Carter 2010, 313).

[60] (May and Marwaha, The Star Gate Archives: Reports of the United States Government Sponsored Psi Program, 1972-1995: Volume 1: Remote Viewing, 1972-1984 2018, 15)

[61] At the height of the Cold War, annual spending was estimated at around $15 billion a year in present-day terms. Taken from http://blogs.reuters.com/great-debate/2010/07/16/us-intelligence-spending-value-for-money/ by Bernd Debusmann, 16 July 2010.

[62] (Swann, Remote Viewing The Real Story 1996).

[63] (Puthoff and Targ, Magnetometer Stability Studies 1975).

[64] Quote attributed to 'a senior CIA official', (Schnabel 1997).

[65] (Targ, Do You See What I See? 2008, 107).

[66] (Puthoff and Targ, Project SCANATE CIA-RDP96-00791 R 000100480002-4 1973).

[67] (Kress 1977).

[68] (Targ, The Reality of ESP 2012, 50-55)

[69] (Puthoff, Targ and Humphrey, et al. 1980, 49).

[70] (Hansen, Schlitz and Tart 1984, 265).

[71] (Dunne and Jahn, Information and Uncertainty in Remote Perception Research 2003).

[72] (Schwartz, Preliminary Report on a Prototype Remote Viewing Methodology in Archaeology 1981).

[73] (Schwartz, Through Time and Space: The Evidence for Remote Viewing n.d.)

[74] (Atwater 2001, 56).

[75] (Puthoff, Targ and Humphrey, et al. 1980)

[76] (J. McMoneagle, The Stargate Chronicles – Memoirs of a Psychic Spy 2002, 109).

[77] As well as in McMoneagle's own The Stargate Chronicles (p 120-124), most recently with photos and sketches in P. H. Smith's The Essential Guide to Remote Viewing 2015, 45-63

[78] (Targ, The Reality of ESP 2012, 134).

[79] (Larson 1984).

[80] (Utts 1996, 23)

[81] (Mumford, Rose and Goslin 1995, 3-64)

[82] (May, The American Institutes for Research Review of the Department of Defense's STAR GATE Program: A Commentary 1996).

[83] (May and Marwaha, The Star Gate Archives: Reports of the United States Government Sponsored Psi Program, 1972-1995: Volume 1: Remote Viewing, 1972-1984 2018, Appendix V Page 511 contains a breakdown of funding by year, and a list of fund sources).

[84] (P. H. Smith, A Review of the A.I.R. Report 1996).

[85] (P. H. Smith, Reading the Enemy's Mind: Inside Star Gate: America's Psychic Espionage Program 2005, 449)

[86] (HRVG n.d.).

[87] (IRVA n.d.)

[88] (Applied Precognition Project n.d.)

[89] (Utts 1996).

Literature

Applied Precognition Project. n.d. *Mission*. Accessed May 2018. http://www.appliedprecog.com/mission.

Atwater, F. H. 2001. *Captain of My Ship Master of My Soul*. Hampton Roads.

Benson, Herbert. 2000. *The Relaxation Response*. HarperCollins.

Bremseth, L.R. (Commander United States Navy). 2001. *Unconventional Human Intelligence Support: Transcendent and Asymmetric Warfare Implications of Remote Viewing*. Quantico, VA: Marine Corps University.

Carter, Jimmy. 2010. *White House Diary*. New York: Farrar, Straus and Giroux.

Cayce, Edgar Evans, and Hugh Lynn Cayce. 2004. *The Outer Limits of Edgar Cayce's Power*. New York: Paraview.

Cox, W.E. 1956. "Precognition: An Analysis. II. Subliminal Precognition." *Journal of the American Society for Psychical Research, 30* 99-109.

Dean, Douglas, John Mihalsky, L. Schroeder, and S. Ostrander. 1974. *Executive ESP*. New York: Prentice-Hall.

Dunne, B., and R. Jahn. 2014. *Consciousness and the Source of Reality: The PEAR Odyssey*. Princeton: ICRL Press.

Dunne, B., and R. Jahn. 2003. "Information and Uncertainty in Remote Perception Research." *Journal of Scientific Exploration, Vol. 17, No. 2* 207–241.

Edwards, Betty. 1979. *Drawing on the Right Side of the Brain*. Tarcher.

Graff, Dale. 2007. "Explorations in Precognitive Dreaming." *Journal for Scientific Exploration (JSE), Vol 21, No. 4* 707-722.

—. 1998. *Tracks in the Psychic Wilderness*. Boston: Element Books.

Graff, Dale, and Patricia S. Cyrus. 2017. "Perceiving the future news: Evidence for retrocausation." *AIP Conference Proceedings 1841, 030001*. AIP Publishing. https://doi.org/10.1063/1.4982772.

Gurney, Edmund, Frederic Myers, and Frank Podmore. 1886. *Phantasms of the Living*. London: Society for Psychical Research.

Hansen, G.P., M.J. Schlitz, and C.T. Tart. 1984. "Remote Viewing Research 1973-1982." In *The Mind Race*, by Russell Targ and Keith Harary, 265. New York: Villard Books.

HeartMath Science and Research. n.d. *HeartMath Science and Research*. Accessed May 2018. https://www.heartmath.com/research/#hrv.

HRVG. n.d. *HRVG Philosophy*. Accessed May 2018. https://hrvg.org/philosophy.php.

IONS. n.d. *IONS Meditation Resources.* Accessed May 2018. http://www.noetic.org/meditation-bibliography/meditation-reources.

IRVA. n.d. *IRVA's Mission and Goals.* Accessed May 2018. http://www.irva.org/remote-viewing/mission.html.

Jung, C. G. 1968. *Collected Works of C. G. Jung, Vol. 9, Part 1. 2nd ed.* Princeton University Press ISBN 0691018332.

Katz, D., and M. Bulgatz. 2013. "Remote Viewers Correctly Predict the Outcome of the 2012 Presidential Election: An expedition into the unexplored territory of remote viewing & rating human subjects as targets, within a binary protocol." *Aperture Magazine, Spring/Summer 2013 Issue* 46 to 56.

Katz, D., I. Grgić, and T. W. Fendley. 2018. "An Ethnographical Assessment of Project Firefly: A Yearlong Endeavor to Create Wealth by Predicting FOREX Currency Moves with Associative Remote Viewing." *Journal of Scientific Exploration, Vol. 32, No. 1*, March: 21–54.

Katz, D., L. Beem, and T.W. Fedley. 2017. "Explorations into Remote Viewing Microscopic Organisms ("The Phage") and the Effects of Biological Scientists' Exposure to Non Local Perception within a Multidisciplinary Approach." *eigth martinis Issue 15*, April: 48-63.

Kirkpatrick, Sidney D. 2001. *Edgar Cayce: An American Prophet.* Riverhead Books.

Kolodziejzyk, Greg. 2013. "Greg Kolodziejzyk's 13-Year Associative Remote Viewing Experiment Results." *The Journal of Parapsychology.*

Kress, Dr. Kenneth A. 1977. "Parapsychology in Intelligence: A Personal Review and Conclusions." *Studies in Intelligence (In-house CIA publication).*

LaMothe, J.D. 1972. *Controlled Offensive Behavior – USSR.* Medical Intelligence Office, Defense Intelligence Agency.

Larson, Erik. 1984. "Did Psychic Powers Give Firm a Killing In the Silver Market? And Did Greed Ruin It All? Californians Switch Over To an Extrasensory Switch." *The Wall Street Journal. New York, October 22, 1984* 1.

Lawrence, T. 1993. "Gathering in the sheep and goats: A meta-analysis of forced-choice sheep/goat ESP studies, 1947-1993." *Proceedings of the Parapsychological Association 36th Annual Convention, Toronto, Canada* 75-86.

Loftus, E.F., and J.C. Palmer. 1974. "Reconstruction of Automobile Destruction: An Example of the Interaction Between Language and Memory." *Journal of Verbal Learning And Verbal Behavior 13* 585-589.

May, E. 1996. "The American Institutes for Research Review of the Department of Defense's STAR GATE Program: A Commentary." *Journal of Scientific Exploration, Vol. 10, No. 1* 89-107.

May, E., and S.B. Marwaha. 2018. *The Star Gate Archives: Reports of the United States Government Sponsored Psi Program, 1972-1995: Volume 1: Remote Viewing, 1972-1984.* McFarland.

May, E., J. Utts, and V. Trask. 1989. *Review of The Psychoenergetic Research Conducted at SRI International (1973-1988).* SRI International.

May, E., V. Rubel, and M Auerbach. 2014. *ESP Wars East & West.* Laboratories for Fundamental Research.

Mayer, Elizabeth Lloyd. 2007. *Extraordinary Knowing.* Bantam Books.

McCraty, R., M. Atkinson, and R.T. Bradley. 2004. "Electrophysiological Evidence of Intuition: Part 1. The Surprising Role of the Heart." *Journal of Alternative and Complementary Medicine* 133-143.

McGilchrist, Iain. 2009. *The Master and His Emissary.* Yale University Press.

McMoneagle, J.W., and E.C. May. 2004. "The Possible Role of Intention, Attention, and Expectation in Remote Viewing." *www.mceagle.com.* www.mceagle.com/remote-viewing/IntentionAttentionExpectation.pdf.

McMoneagle, Joe. 2000. *Remote Viewing Secrets.* Hampton Roads.

—. 2002. *The Stargate Chronicles – Memoirs of a Psychic Spy.* Hampton Roads.

Morris, Douglas A. 2010. *Anomalous Human Cognition: A Possible Role within the Crucible of Intelligence Collection.* National Defense Intelligence College.

Mumford, Michael D., Andrew M. Rose, and David A. Goslin. 1995. *An Evaluation of Remote Viewing: Research and Applications.* Washington, D.C.: American Institutes for Research.

Ostrander, S., and L. Schroeder. 1970. *Psychic Discoveries Behind the Iron Curtain.* Prentice Hall.

Palmer, John. 2017. "Experimenter Effects." *Psi Encyclopedia.* July. Accessed February 2018. https://psi-encyclopedia.spr.ac.uk/articles/experimenter-effects.

Puryear, Herbert. 1982. *The Edgar Cayce Primer: Discovering the Path to Self-Transformation.* Bantan Books.

Puthoff, H. 1996. "CIA-Initiated Remote Viewing Program at Stanford Research Institute." *Journal of Scientific Exploration, Vol. 10, No. 1* 63-76.

—. 2015. "Keynote speech IRVA Conference."

Puthoff, H. 1984. *RV Reliability, Enhancement, and Evaluation.* SRI International.

Puthoff, H., and R. Targ. 1976. "A Perceptual Channel for Information Transfer Over Kilometer Distances: Historical Perspective and Recent Research." *Proceedings of the IEEE 64* 329-54.

Puthoff, H., and R. Targ. 1974. "Information Transmission Under Conditions Of Sensory Shielding." *Nature (252)* 602-607.

Puthoff, H., and R. Targ. 1975. *Magnetometer Stability Studies.* Proposal, Menlo Park, CA: SRI International.

—. 2005. *Mind-Reach: Scientists Look at Psychic Abilities.* Hampton Roads.

Puthoff, H., and R. Targ. 1973. *Project SCANATE CIA-RDP96-00791 R 000100480002-4.* Menlo Park, CA: SRI International.

Puthoff, H., R. Targ, and C. T. Tart. 1979. *Resolution in remote viewing studies: Mini-targets.* Research in Parapsychology, pp. 120-122.

Puthoff, H., R. Targ, and E. May. 1979. *Direct perception of remote geographic locations.* New York: Praeger.

Puthoff, H., R. Targ, B. Humphrey, and E. May. 1980. *Special Orientation Techniques CIA-RDP96-00788R001300170001-0.* Menlo Park, CA: SRI International.

Radin, Dean. 2004. "Electrodermal Presentiments of Future Emotions." *Journal of Scientific Exploration, Vol. 18, No. 2* 253-273.

—. 2006. *Entangled Minds.* New York: Paraview.

—. 2013. *Supernormal.* New York: Crown Publishing.

Rhine, J.B. 1934. *Extra-Sensory Perception.*

Rhine, J.B., G. Pratt, and C. Stuart. 1940. *Extra-Sensory Perception after Sixty Years.* Holt.

Roney-Dougal, S.M., and J. Solfvin. 2011. "Exploring the relationship between Tibetan meditation attainment and precognition." *Journal of Scientific Exploration, 24* 29–46.

Roney-Dougal, S.M., and J. Solfvin. 2006. "Yogic attainment in relation to awareness of precognitive targets." *Journal of Parapsychology, 70* 91–120.

Roney-Dougal, S.M., J. Solfvin, and J. Fox. 2008. "An exploration of degree of meditation attainment in relation to psychic awareness with Tibetan Buddhists." *Journal of Scientific Exploration* 161–178.

Roser, M.E., and M.S. Gazzaniga. 2007. "The Interpreter in Human Psychology." *Plymouth University.* Accessed Mar 2017. www.psy.plymouth.ac.uk.

Schlitz, M., and C. Honorton. 1992. "A ganzfeld ESP study within an artistically gifted population." *Journal of the American Society for Psychical Research, 86* 83-98.

Schlitz, M., and E. Gruber. 1980. "Transcontinental Remote Viewing." *Journal of Parapsychology, 44* 305-317.

Schnabel, Jim. 1997. *Remote Viewers: The Secret History of America's Psychic Spies.* New York: Dell Publishing.

Schwartz, Stephan. n.d. *A Partial Meditation Bibliography 2006-2009.* http://www.stephanaschwartz.com/partial-meditation-bibliography/.

—. 2007. *Opening to the Infinite.* Nemoseen Media.

—. 2017. *Remote Viewing.* January. https://psi-encyclopedia.spr.ac.uk/articles/remote-viewing.

—. 1981. "Preliminary Report on a Prototype Remote Viewing Methodology in Archaeology." *Research in Parapsychology*, 25-27.

—. 2001. *The Alexandria Project.* iUniverse.com.

—. 2001. *The Secret Vaults of Time.* iUniverse.com.

—. n.d. "Through Time and Space: The Evidence for Remote Viewing." *academia.edu.* www.academia.edu/9540484/Through_Time_and_Space_The_Evidence_for_Remote_Viewing.

—. n.d. "Two Application-Oriented Experiments Employing a Submarine Involving a Novel Remote Viewing Protocol, One Testing the ELF Hypothesis." *academia.edu.* www.academia.edu/29933077/Two_Application-Oriented_Experiments_Employing_a_Submarine_Involving_a_Novel_Remote_Viewing_Protocol_One_Testing_the_ELF_Hypothesis.

Schwartz, Stephan, and R. J. De Matte. 1982. "The Mobius Psi-Q Test: Report on a Mass Precognition Experiment With Correlates." *Stephan A. Schwartz.* www.stephanaschwartz.com.

Sherwood, S.J., and C. A. Roe. 2003. "A Review of Dream ESP Studies Conducted Since the Maimonides Dream ESP Programme." *Journal of Consciousness Studies, 10, No. 6–7* 85–109.

Smith, C. C., D. Laham, and G. Moddel. 2014. "Stock Market Prediction Using Associative Remote Viewing by Inexperienced Remote Viewers." *Journal of Scientific Exploration, Vol. 28, No. 1* 7–16.

Smith, Paul H. 1996. "A Review of the A.I.R. Report." *Remote Viewing Instructional Services.* http://www.irva.org/library/pdfs/smith1996air1.pdf.

—. 1986. *Coordinate Remote Viewing Training Manual.* Defense Intelligence Agency.

—. 2005. *Reading the Enemy's Mind: Inside Star Gate: America's Psychic Espionage Program.* New York: Forge.

—. 2015. *The Essential Guide to Remote Viewing.* Las Vegas: Intentional Press.

Smith, Paul H., and et al. 1986. *Coordinate Remote Viewing Training Manual.* Procedural, Defense Intelligence Agency.

Storm, Lance, and Patrizio E. Tressoldi. 2017. "Gathering in more sheep and goats: A meta-analysis of forced choice sheep-goat ESP studies, 1994-2015." *Journal of the Society for Psychical Research, 81(2)* 79-107.

Storm, Lance, Patrizio E. Tressoldi, and Lorenzo Di Risio. 2010. "Meta-Analysis of Free-Response Studies, 1992–2008 Assessing the Noise Reduction Model in Parapsychology." *Psychological Bulletin Vol. 136, No. 4* 471– 485.

Swann, Ingo. 1998. *Penetration.* Ingo Swann Books.

Swann, Ingo. 2002. "Remote Viewing Processes and Layers of Meaning." *reprinted in eight martinis Issue 3 March 2010* 12-17.

—. 1996. "Remote Viewing The Real Story." *academia.edu.* www.academia.edu/31649905/REMOTE_VIEWING_Memoir_by_Ing o_Swann.

Swann, Ingo. 1995. "The 1973 Remote Viewing Probe of the Planet Jupiter." *reprinted in eight martinis Issue 4 August 2010* 37-43.

—. 1995. "The Emergence of Project "Scanate"." 12.

Talbot, Michael. 1991. *The Holographic Universe.* Harper Perennial.

Targ, Russell. 2008. *Do You See What I See?* Hampton Roads.

—. n.d. *ESP Trainer by Russell Targ.* Accessed May 2018. http://www.espresearch.com/iphone/.

—. 2004. *Limitless Mind.* New World Library.

Targ, Russell. 1996. "Remote Viewing at Stanford Research Institute in the 1970's A Memoir." *Society for Scientific Exploration* 77-88.

—. 2012. *The Reality of ESP.* Wheaton, IL: Quest Books.

Targ, Russell, Jane Katra, Dean Brown, and Wenden Wiegand. 1995. "Viewing the Future: A Pilot Study with an Error-Detecting Protocol." *Journal of Scientific Exploration* (Society for Scientific Exploration) 9 (3): 374. www.scientificexploration.org.

Ullman, M., S. Krippner, and A. Vaughan. 1989. *Dream Telepathy: Experiments in Nocturnal ESP.* McFarland.

Utts, Jessica. 1996. "An Assessment of the Evidence for Psychic Functioning." *Journal of Scientific Exploration, Vol. 10, No. 1* 3-30.

Walsh, K., & Moddel, G. 2007. "Effect of Belief on Psi Performance on a Card Guessing Task." *Journal of Scientific Exploration, 21* 501-510.

Watt, Caroline. 1988. "Characteristics of successful free-response targets: Theoretical considerations." *Proceedings of the 31st Annual Convention of the Parapsychological Association* 247-263.

Acknowledgement and Thanks

Thanks to all those mentioned in this guide, as well as the many unnamed who contributed to the efforts discussed.

Special thanks to Russell Targ, Stephan Schwartz, Skip Atwater, Henry Reed, and Paul H. Smith for imparting their wisdom. Thanks to Jessica Utts, Dale Graff, Nancy Smith, and Christopher Barbour for being so accommodating in answering my questions and allowing me to use their words.

Thanks to Rachel Khona and Tyler Coburn for use of their first-timer remote viewing sessions.

Too many to thank here, but there are several individuals and organizations working to promote remote viewing and encouraging viewers; included amongst these are IRVA, APP, Daz Smith, Dick Allgire, The Farsight Institute, Alexis Poquiz, Teresa Frisch and the moderators and active members at the TKR Forum - the remote viewing community is enriched by their efforts.

Thanks to the members of the RVPGNYC who show me, in every meeting, that there is more to our physical reality than meets the eye.

Thanks also to Mary Crosby, Penny and Paul Day, Debra Katz, Mary Krombel, Paul H. Smith, Paul O'Connor, Joyce Wahlberg, Linda Rae Reneau and Doron Ariel Shpasser for their valuable comments and suggestions which greatly improved this book.

Lastly, my appreciation to those who bought the first edition and those who provided feedback and suggestions.

About the Author

 Since experiencing remote viewing for himself in a week-long conference with pioneers Russell Targ and Stephan Schwartz in 2010, Jon has made it a mission to promote the practice and introduce it to others.

To help spread the word he started a remote viewing practice group in 2011, with the goal of providing an open and friendly environment in which to discuss and practise remote viewing. The group continues to meet regularly in Manhattan, NYC.

Instructed by many of remote viewing luminaries, as well as Targ and Schwartz, including Skip Atwater, and Paul H. Smith, Jon is an advocate of all forms of RV.

Jon runs *Focal Point*, IRVA's online target practice programme. In May 2018 Jon was elected to the board of the International Remote Viewing Association.

Printed in Great Britain
by Amazon

55990682R00116